With Many Voices:
Liturgies in Contexts

Reimagining Church as Event: Perspectives from the Margins
Series Editors: George Zachariah and Sudipta Singh

In these eleven volumes, a collective of Indian theologians envisions Church as an Event that happens in particular contexts in the life of the communities at the margins. They argue that in the life of the communities who experience on their bodies the violence and hegemony of dominant power relations, morality, and religious dogmas and practices, the church happens as countercultural experiences that disrupt the logic of the prevailing order. These experiences enable and empower them to affirm and celebrate their differences, knowledges and beauty even as they weave their liberation. Church as event is a call to rising to life, creating life-flourishing communities that live out the foretaste of the reign of God.

Titles in this Series

Church and Religious Diversity Joshua Samuel and Samuel Mall
Church and Gender Justice Aruna Gnanadason
Faith in the Age of Empire Y.T. Vinayaraj
Dalitekklesia: A Church from Below Raj Bharat Patta
Church and Climate Justice Vinod Wesley
Church and Disability Samuel George
Church and Diakonia in the Age of COVID-19 Mothy Varkey
Decolonising Oikoumene Gladson Jathanna
Church and Human Sexuality Arvind Theodore
With Many Voices: Liturgies in Context Viji Varghese Eapen (Ed.)
The Word becoming Flesh George Zachariah

With Many Voices: Liturgies in Contexts

Viji Varghese Eapen

(Editor)

2020

With Many Voices: Liturgies in Contexts - jointly published by the Indian Society for Promoting Christian Knowledge (ISPCK), Post Box 1585, Kashmere Gate, Delhi-110006 and Council for World Mission, Singapore-338729.

ISBN: 978-93-88945-88-2

Kindle Edition: 978-93-88945-99-8

Cover Illustration Credit : Immanuel Paul Vivekanandh K

Laser typeset by

ISPCK, Post Box 1585, 1654, Madarsa Road, Kashmere Gate, Delhi-110006 • *Tel:* 23866323

e-mail: ashish@ispck.org.in • ella@ispck.org.in
website: www.ispck.org.in

Contents

LITURGICAL RESOURCES

Foreword

DISCERNMENT AND RADICAL ENGAGEMENT (DARE) is an initiative of the Council for World Mission (CWM) to enable faith communities to *clarify what it means to engage in* public witness to God's justice and peace in a corrupt and conflicted world.

> The mission of DARE is conceived as the coming together of (a) the *radical soul* of discernment and sense-making in theology and biblical criticism; (b) the yearnings for *signifying engagement* that rise out of the slums of modernism and the valleys of despair; and (c) the commitment to redemption songs that *inspire disturbance* at the hubs of power.

As part of the DARE initiative, each region of the CWM is invited to prepare and share biblical and theological resources on current themes and issues being considered by the CWM, drawing upon the experiences and resources from the region.

Interfaith Engagement, Ecumenism and Inclusive communities against dehumanising social categorisations are the themes for the book series undertaken by the South Asia region of the CWM. The thrust is centred on **Reimagining Church as Event: Perspectives from the Margins**. It calls to the fore, persons living in the margins and highlights their voice, their narratives and their passion for a rearrangement of life in communities, as we know it, and a commitment to rise to life and to break out from Babylon. These books are intended for the use of laypeople, pastors and evangelists as well as for theological students and seminaries. The series offer stories and narratives, analyses, liturgical resources, biblical, theological and ethical reflections, and missional/praxis proposals.

Church is an event that happens at the margins of contemporary life. Church happens as an epiphanic event where the divine presence is manifested and experienced in the pathos, struggles, contestations and harmonies of everyday existence. Church happens in those spaces where we celebrate the presence of Jesus, the Christ, in the flourishing of life. Church happens when we are transformed by one another, and inspired and enabled to engage in the transformative politics of the reign of God. Church happens whenever and wherever spirit-filled communities reclaim their subversive moral agency and contest the logic and practices of domination and exclusion. Church happens when the community experiences the healing power of the wounded healer and join Jesus in this risk-taking mission, despite the wounds we bear. To reimagine, the Church requires courage and commitment to engage in the mission of nurturing and organising communities of resistance and healing. This book series is a humble attempt at exposing and encouraging this radical expression of Church.

I appreciate and thank all those who are associated with this series, the authors, the contributors, the publishers and the editors. I commend this book series in the hope and prayers that they will help the faith communities in South Asia, and beyond, to *discern God's presence in communities and dare to engage* in ways that re-present the God of life in communities and the public square, *Rising to Life: Living out the New Heaven and New Earth.*

Colin Cowan
General Secretary
Council for World Mission

Introduction

*Cláudio Carvalhaes**

It is with great joy that I write an introduction to this book, which is part of a larger project of liturgies in contexts where the life of the Church is marked by the presence of God in the creation of the real liturgical work of the people.

This book carries the gifts of prayers and orders of worship from people who are wrestling with their faith in historical contexts, reimagining the very life of the Church as an event from below, feeling and breathing with people in their daily lives.

The Church of Jesus Christ should be understood as a daily living of a community that worships God, breathes together its prayers and songs and gestures, breaks bread around a common table, cares for each other, mends what is broken, sustains what is threatened to be ripped apart and holds on to life as a fragile gift of God that is so often susceptible to be taken away. Church is about life together, keeping people alive, generating honour to each other and protecting one another from violence.

Moreover, the Church in its worship form is the manifestation of an event, a daily or weekly miracle that, when happening in the community, has the promise that something will happen!

Church as an event happens when people gather to worship God and are transformed by the "renewal of our minds." Church as an event is the manifestation of the Holy Spirit visiting the community and bringing healing, empowering and sustenance to its people. Church as an event is like a signpost to the world, pointing to the direction of life, avoiding so many paths of death. Church as an event is a true happening in the life of a community being oriented by God to a new life and in this relation, a life also offered to the world. Church as an event is the fullness of God's glory in the bodies of people, putting in their hearts the desire to live a life of solidarity, filling them with blessings, and marking the incarnation of the Jesus life with the fruits of the Spirit. Church as an event takes the daily life of the people as its main source of theological insights and from the living together that happens on the streets, we find the collective breathing that sustains each other. Thus, starting from where life happens, the event of worship becomes the highest event of faith in the life of a community.

In this book, we can see and feel the Church happening in various contexts in the language being created from where the struggle is happening, naming injustice and calling for God's justice. From each place, the power of life bursting into prayers and songs can be felt and will open ways for other communities to pair their own lives with each community here represented. The liturgies of this book do not resign us to death nor to the impossibility of explaining why death looms large so intensely around our people. Instead, these liturgies face the complicit reality of death, the erosion of language, the abandonment of those suffering, the pain of so many, and the growing sense that we are incapable of changing anything in the oppressive structures of the world.

These liturgies offer something new. They recover buried forms of memories that will renew the strength that comes from the connection that people hold to their locations, creating practices that will sustain the bodies of believers and their historical processes of transformation.

Today's world is filled with evil manifestations: fascism, patriarchy, wars, ecological destruction, prejudices, and social inequality. We are all losing the already meagre sources to survive. More and more, we need communities to pray with others, to sing together, to share a meal, to be anointed and to heal, to prophesy and to keep the world going. In these liturgies, people do not deny the world's pain, do not normalise the threats of violence and do not shrug their shoulders with apathy before forceful agents of death. Instead, people take into account the depersonalisation of individuals and restore a sense of self from a collective understanding of a body, the body of Christ.

These liturgies tell us of the power of collective memory that can restore in us a new heart, help us think otherwise and live the gospel in ways that we have not yet lived. These liturgies bring joy where there is no joy, healing where there is hurt, and an affirmation of life where there is only condemnation to death.

Each liturgical context shows the power and the ingenuity of people who, when staying together, create the conditions of possibilities of life to continue. These liturgies expand books of prayers with vibrant collections of prayers and life pulsing at every line. They show us the paradoxes of life so that we avoid the temptation of praying or singing too glibly. These prayers demand a covenant with God and one another. These liturgies push us against resignation and exhaustion, fear and hopelessness. With each liturgy, we find ourselves singing with others and for those who cannot sing, praying with each other and for those who cannot pray. Together, a whole powerful community is represented within these liturgies.

The Council for World Mission, under the leadership of Sudipta Singh, has inaugurated a new way of doing liturgies: not from universal claims but from local cries. It is from local cries that Christians can claim the love of God everywhere and honour the suffering of others, which affects us all as Christians. In these prayers, we are imbricated and are part of each person's suffering. To pray these liturgies is to pray with all who are suffering.

I thank God for this wonderful initiative and for the Church to actually live what liturgy is all about: the work of the people, all the people, with God.

***Dr. Cláudio Carvalhaes** serves the Union Theological Seminary, New York City, as Associate Professor of Worship.

Marginality and Manyness:
Liturgical Hermeneutics towards
"Church as Event"

Viji Varghese Eapen

Worship that legitimizes classism, racism, casteism, and sexism is dehumanizing and alienating. True worship is that which liberates and calls people to wholeness.[1]

Margaret Shanthi

Will it mean merely being confined to bringing out the meaning of texts, or occasionally protecting them from "wayward" misreading? Or would one implication be that when the moment dawns on us faithfulness will require us the courage to be "prepared" to give up the very text themselves?[2]

Michael N. Jagessar and Stephen Burns

In Ezekiel 37, in "the vision of the valley of dry bones," we see an "epiclesis" that transforms the dry bones into a new humanity. The new community thus formed is part of an event; the bones coming and becoming together, the ribs reinforcing, the skulls reattaching, the sinews and the flesh coming up upon them, and the skin covering them above, the four winds sweeping down from all the four directions and passing through the lifeless creatures, empowering them to stand upon their feet, a vast multitude, an exceptionally extensive army.

To liturgically reread this vision, adopting the words of Margaret Shanthi, is to say that the churches that have become a valley of dehumanised and alienated dry bones, owing to the sins of classism, racism, casteism and sexism, demand not for an act of worship that liturgically legitimises these sins, but which liberates and calls people to wholeness. This is a radical call, as Michael N. Jagessar and Stephen Burns say, a call that is neither limited to bringing out the meaning of texts nor occasionally protecting them from "wayward" misreading, but that urges a commitment and courage to be "prepared" to give up the very text themselves.

Paul Avis, an Anglican theologian and ecumenist, might have conceived the same vision as he remarked that the Church should become new humanity, thus truly human, living in true community, instead of what it is today, a "visibly fragmented, morally compromised, often dysfunctional" institution.[3] Avis' dream reminds us that the *kairos* moment has come afresh for another reimagination—a reimagination of Church as event.

The Council for World Mission, through its initiative, "Discernment and Radical Engagement" (DARE), dares to reimagine Church as event.

> The Church happens as an epiphanic event where the divine presence is manifested and experienced in the pathos, struggles, contestations and harmonies of everyday existence. Church happens in those spaces where and when we are at ease in the presence of the radically Other, where the truth is told in a revealing way, and captives are set free. Here we are transformed by one another, and shaped into companions and conspirators as we engage in the radical politics of the reign of God. Church happens whenever and wherever spirit-filled communities

reclaim their subversive moral agency, and contest the logic and practices of domination and exclusion.[4]

This ecclesiological reimagination of Church as Event invites our attention to a new epistemology and new missiology. The epistemological foundation of this reimagined ecclesiology is not the universal (Church as the mystical Body of Christ) nor the local (Church as local denominations) but rather the intersectional, where we meet and are met by "the other," transformed by each other and shaped together for a radical engagement. Further, this ecclesiology, Church as Event, rediscovers the exact mission of the Church—to become companions and conspirators and engage as a subversive moral agency in the radical politics of the reign of God.

These ecclesiological and missiological perspectives are obvious in George Zachariah's elaboration of the theme of Church becoming an event, as he critiques the dominant model of "Church as a house" with "Church as a street." The dominant ecclesiological model of "Church as a house" directs us to our practices of exclusion such as liturgy, sacraments, scripture, priesthood, sacred places and moral codes that provide the identity to the Church, which includes security, social acceptance and power.

> The model of House is a dominant model for Church that we see in our ecclesiological discourses. The house provides us a sense of identity by virtue of being part of the household. We don't have to earn it; it is given to us. It offers us security, social acceptance, and power. When we look at Church as house, it has its own liturgy, sacraments, scripture, priesthood, sacred places, and moral codes. The social acceptance and the cultural capital of the Church lure us to consider taking membership in the Church not only as a symbol of pride and status, but also as a wise investment. The identity of the house is determined by the fortified walls that keep the Other away from it. Said differently, it

is our practices of exclusion which provide the house its identity. So house is a symbol of exclusion. Our supremacy and honor are mediated through our practices of exclusion which discursively constructs the Other as impure, shameful, and inferior.[5]

In contrast, Zachariah proposes the model of "Church as a street," a symbol of mutuality and relationality. "Church as a street" happens "as fellowship, solidarity, love, care, compassion, justice, and restoration in the lives of people who go through the tragic experience of utter God-forsakenness."[6] As he attempts a radical ecclesiological reimagination through the image of the street, he says,

> Street is the abode of those who are thrown out from their homes. Street is also the home of those who are denied entry into those houses guarded by barbed wire fencing and security personnel. It is in the street that the "homeless" has redefined the concept and practice of "home." Hence the street invites us to experience the happening of Church in the most unexpected places. Is it possible for us to get out of the security and sacredness of the idolized Church to become part of the great experience of the Church happening in the street?[7]

However, the question is whether one could attempt an ecclesiological reimagination without a liturgical reimagination, primarily because of liturgy's two-way connectedness with the Church. Firstly, as the Orthodox liturgist Baby Varghese says, "Liturgy is the self-affirmation of the Church, the manifestation of her very being."[8] Liturgical theologians such as Bryan D. Spinks and John R. K. Fenwick also believe that the liturgy expresses what we believe and reflect the language, thought-forms and priorities of the age in which they were created.[9] These liturgists insist upon the ontological function of the liturgy in its relationship with the Church. Secondly, as J. R. Macphail, an Anglican theologian argues, liturgy "purges the conscience" to transform the Church to be apostolic, missionary and united.[10] The idea that liturgy shapes the conscience of the Church is an idea which dominated even during the colonial era; one instance is the statement that "liturgy moulds the church; the church, in large measure at least, moulds the nation; and the nation, queen and mistress as she is of kingdoms, contributes instrumentally more than any other power to mould the world."[11] These scholars assert the praxiological aspect of any liturgy in transforming the Church.

Accordingly, the new ecclesiology suggested by the CWM demands us to explore the nature and scope of a new liturgy that ontologically expresses "Church as event" as well as praxiologically allows the Church to live as event. In other words, one of the theological tasks to realise this new ecclesiology is to venture into a corresponding liturgical renaissance with the same epistemological and missiological foci. However, such a liturgical reimagination is not possible without a relevant liturgical hermeneutics, a hermeneutics based on a dialectical and dialogical subjective realisation and revelation of the participating active agents rather than based on *fides quaerens intellectum* (faith seeking understanding).

Methodology

Can there be a liturgical reimagination without a liturgical deconstruction, and if so, to what extent? Further, what does it mean to deconstruct liturgies if their basic structure is "determined," "fixed" and "given" to the Church by the Lord and/or His disciples? And, most importantly, has liturgy ever had a specific unified pattern or shape, and if so, how far does that help today's Church to remain relevant to the multiple experiences of many voices from the margins, subordinated on the basis of class, caste, race, gender, ethnicity, etc.? To answer these questions, this article takes a postmodern and postcolonial approach, particularly juxtaposing Paul F. Bradshaw's application of the postmodern "hermeneutics of suspicion" of liturgical historiography and Gayatri Chakravorty Spivak's postcolonial "hermeneutics of homework" of subaltern historiography.

Liturgical Studies: From "Tree" to "Rhizome"

According to Teresa Berger, liturgical developments have never remained untouched by the critical developments, resulting in at least four methodological shifts in liturgical studies:

(i)   towards "a deepened appreciation of liturgy as a multi-textured practice;"

(ii) towards reading liturgical texts "as a 'living literature' with a quite complicated relationship with the past they embody;"

(iii) towards "a more comprehensive understanding of liturgical practices that includes not only the key sacramental rites, but ecclesial rituals;"

(iv) towards an interrogation of the cultural, geographical and geopolitical context of worship.[12]

These shifts in liturgical studies were fuelled generally by the twentieth-century developments in the area of social sciences, and particularly by postmodern trends. According to Graham Ward, while modernity was a period governed by highly determined forms such as the circle, the cube, the spiral, even the double helix, postmodernity was a condition (rather than a period) that gained expression in indeterminate forms such as rhizome.[13] Ward employs images of trees (vertical "arboreal" structures with firm root structures) and rhizomes (a horizontal network of randomly connected roots) to differentiate modern and postmodern cultures. He is informed by the French thinkers Gilles Deleuze and Felix Guattari, who have developed the image of "tree" and "rhizome" to differentiate cultures. For them, rhizomes, unlike trees, are not reducible to the one or the multiple, composed not of units but dimensions, or rather directions in motion, with no beginning or end, but a middle, from which it grows and which it overspills.

> [...] unlike trees or their roots, the rhizome connects any point to any other point, and its traits are not necessarily linked to traits of the same nature; it brings into play very different regimes of signs, and even nonsign states. The rhizome is reducible neither to the One nor the multiple. It is not the One that becomes Two or even directly three, four, five, etc. It is not a multiple derived from the One, or to which One is added (n + 1). It is composed not of units but of dimensions, or rather directions in motion. It has neither beginning nor end, but always middle (milieu) from which it grows and which it overspills. It constitutes linear multiplicities with n dimensions having neither subject nor object, which can be laid out on a plane of consistency, and from which the One is always subtracted (n - 1). When a multiplicity of this kind changes dimension, it necessarily changes in nature as well, undergoes a metamorphosis. Unlike a structure, which is defined by a set of points and positions, with binary relations between the points and bi-univocal relationships between the positions, the rhizome is made only of lines: lines of segmentarity and stratification as its dimensions, and the line of flight or de-territorialization as the maximum dimension after which the multiplicity undergoes metamorphosis, changes in nature. These lines, or lineaments, should not be confused with lineages of the arborescent type, which are merely localizable linkages between points and positions. Unlike the tree, the rhizome is not the object of reproduction: neither external reproduction as image-tree nor internal reproduction as tree-structure. The rhizome is an anti-genealogy. It is a short-term memory, or anti-memory. The rhizome operates by variation, expansion,

conquest, capture, offshoots. Unlike the graphic arts, drawing, or photography, unlike tracings, the rhizome pertains to a map that must be produced, constructed, a map that is always detachable, connectable, reversible, modifiable, and has multiple entryways and exits and its own lines of flight. It is tracings that must be put on the map, not the opposite. In contrast to centered (even polycentric) systems with hierarchical modes of communication and pre-established paths, the rhizome is an acentered, non-hierarchical, non-signifying system without a General and without an organizing memory or central automaton, defined solely by a circulation of states. What is at question in the rhizome is a relation to sexuality—but also to the animal, the vegetal, the world, politics, the book, things natural and artificial—that is totally different from the arborescent relation: all manner of "becomings."[14]

Nathan Mitchell, and more importantly, Berger, applies rhizomatic images as an optic/lens to study the liturgical history, as she argues that it provides an alternative to other lenses such as those of an organic development or an evolution of liturgical rites in liturgical historiography.[15] While, liturgical historiography in evolutionist terms assumes that the following liturgical elements have branched out vertically from the root elements, a rhizomatic optic conceives this development as a growth that has happened through multiple, horizontal, nonlinear, and quite random circulations. For Berger, Bradshaw who moves away from "a narrative of neatly linear development of liturgy toward an acknowledgement of starkly fragmentary, disparate, and localized nature of the extant evidence" appears to (re)read the liturgical development using this rhizomatic lens. Such liturgical historiography proves that the basic structure of the early liturgies was not monolithic, that was "determined", "fixed" and "given".

Bradshaw and "Hermeneutics of Suspicion"

Employing the rhizomatic lens, Bradshaw's postmodern methodology questions the "previous certainties and a sense of a historiographic master narrative," as he critically engages with the philological, structural and organic (as well as comparative) approaches, which he considers have been naively attempted to formulate principles for the interpretation of primary liturgical sources, and emphatically asserts the vitality of employing the hermeneutics of suspicion.[16]

> [...] even the historiography of Christian Worship cannot but be shaped by broader intellectual trends, postmodern formations included. An example may be found in the work of Paul F. Bradshaw, who in a range of scholarly publications spanning the last 30 years, has rewritten the history of the early centuries of Christian worship as we knew it. His methodological principles, seemingly generated simply by a fresh, careful rereading of the sources themselves, nevertheless bear the stamp of their time, in this case a telling affinity to postmodern theories of knowledge. Leaving behind both previous certainties and a sense of a historiographic master narrative, Bradshaw, in the preface to the 2002 edition of his *The Search for the Origins of Christian Worship*, emphasizes his conversation that "we know much, much less about the liturgical practices of the first three centuries of Christianity than we once thought that we did. [...] Bradshaw outlines the development of his own interpretive strategies, essentially mapping, in conversation with earlier approaches, his move away from a narrative of neatly linear development toward an acknowledgement of the starkly fragmentary and disparate nature of the extant evidence, and its radically local character. Bradshaw stresses the need for a "hermeneutic of suspicion" [..]. [17]

The adherents of the philological method treated liturgical texts like other ancient manuscripts, comparing variant readings and trying to arrive at the original that lay beneath them all.[18]

Critiquing this method, Bradshaw argues that, on the one hand, the early liturgical manuscripts were "living literature," "material which circulates within a community and forms a part of its heritage and tradition but which is constantly subject to revision and rewriting to reflect changing historical and cultural circumstances."[19] On the other hand, he advises us concerning some liturgical texts being "liturgical debris," those "primitive and venerable texts copied into later collections of material just because they were primitive and venerable, and not because of any real intention of putting them into practice."[20] While the early Christians knew what texts were to be used or not to be used, the modern scholars are left to assume it.

According to Gregory Dix, the fourfold action of the Eucharist rite—the offertory, the prayer, the fraction and the communion—reproduced from the original "seven-action scheme" of the Eucharist rite, i.e., (i) took bread, (ii) gave thanks over it, (iii) broke it (iv) distributed it, saying certain words; (v) took a cup (vi) gave thanks over that (vii) handed it to His disciples, saying certain words, was the single liturgical shape of the Eucharist with "absolute unanimity."[21] Bradshaw argues that such premises have been built on "unreliable foundations."[22] Refuting the structural approach of Dix, Bradshaw says that the early Christian worship was not "nearly so fixed or uniform" but "pluriform in doctrine and practice," and hence, the development of Christian worship was mostly a movement from considerable differences over quite fundamental elements to an increasing amalgamation and standardisation of local customs.[23] Bradshaw cites Robert Taft, who in his attempt to locate the evolution of the Byzantine Eucharist within the larger context of liturgical history, refers to four stages of ritual history. Among those stages, according to Taft, the third stage was a period of unification which evolved through the survival of the fittest (and not necessarily of the best), stimulated by the changing ecclesiological and ecclesiastical landscapes, which indeed points to the manyness of liturgies in their original settings.

> [...] what was once one loose collection of individual local churches each with its own liturgical uses, evolved into a series of intermediate structures or federations (later called patriarchates) grouped around certain major sees. This process stimulated a corresponding unification and standardizing of church practice, liturgical and otherwise. Hence, the process of formation of rites is not one of diversification, as is usually held, but of unification. And what one finds in extant rites today, is not a synthesis of all that went before, but rather the result of a selective evolution the survival of the fittest- of the fittest, not necessarily of the best.[24]

Liturgists like Anton Baumstark advocate the organic approach (based upon the comparative method) applying the model of a "living organism," derived by comparative linguists and the other practitioners of the comparative sciences of culture, that utilises a method of "systematic comparison and consequent classification based on a supposed line of descent from the origin of the species."[25] For him, from the resources available for examination, it is crucial "to test for an intrinsic conformity to patterns governed by laws," whether they exist, and to what extent they exist.[26] According to this organic approach, liturgy develops as an organism following a peculiar pattern, from simple and diverse to a complicated and uniform structure. Hence, it is possible to establish previous patterns depending upon the comparison of later evidence. For Bradshaw, this heuristic principle is "observable tendencies" in the growth of liturgies, and he states that one cannot judge a liturgical phenomenon "primitive," solely because it exhibits variety, and "late," merely because it displays prolixity.[27] However, Bradshaw does not dismiss the potential of the comparative method, although, he says that it works better for periods especially after the development of actual liturgical texts, i.e. when there is abundant historical data, rather than during the first three or four centuries.[28]

Critiquing the philological, structural and organic (comparative) approaches which seem to be uncritical about the primary liturgical sources, Bradshaw argues that one should approach the particular character of the text, the author's aims and intentions in its composition, and the context in which it was written, only with a hermeneutics of suspicion. Expounding on Bradshaw's approach, Berger says that a reading of his methodological principles needs to be located within the broader framework of postmodern emphasis on fragmentariness, the mediations of textual representations, discontinuity and difference.

> [...] what earliest liturgical sources might claim for themselves (their apostolic origin being the most obvious example) and highlights the silences, absences, and aporias the historian encounters in these sources. He cautions against the assumptions that texts simply mean what they purport to say, and instead encourages historians of liturgy to ask what might have engendered something being said in the first place and what function the text might have had. [...] With such methodological principles, Bradshaw finds himself in the midst of what drives postmodern historical analyses: an emphasis on fragmentariness, the mediations of textual representations, discontinuity, and difference. Such a reading of Bradshaw's methodological principles does not [...] in anyway negate his findings and re-readings of the origins of Christian worship. Rather, such reading simply suggests how these findings are produced under the conditions of the author's own times.[29]

Predicting the limits of historical science, Bradshaw cautions the need to be aware of being too ready to draw the following conclusions: (i) that authoritative-sounding statements are always genuinely authoritative; (ii) that liturgical legislation is evidence of actual practice; (iii) that when a variety of explanations exist for the origin of a practice, one of them must be genuine.[30] Firstly, he disestablishes the bases and absolute claims that several liturgical practices that had emerged quite early in the life of the Church rapidly reached normative or universal status. Secondly, he asserts that it does not mean that liturgical legislation was recognised everywhere or ever put into practice anywhere at all, merely because an authoritative body had made that regulation. Thirdly, concerning the original purpose and meaning of any liturgical practice, the fact that there were multiple explanations and interpretations show that no authoritative tradition had survived. All these arguments by Bradshaw, based on the "hermeneutics of suspicion," deconstruct earlier philological, structural, organic and comparative approaches, and the claims of unity and linearity of several fragments in the evolution of liturgical rites.[31]

Bradshaw Contested: Perspectives from South Asia—Marginality and Manyness

Bradshaw employs the "hermeneutics of suspicion," which interrogates the cultural, geographical and geopolitical context of worship to provide a deepened appreciation of liturgy as a multitextured practice, to deconstruct the liturgical historiography of Judaeo-Christian liturgy developed in the Graeco-Roman context. However, for "Church as event," ecclesiology in the South Asian, mainly Indian, context, what concerns is not merely how the liturgies originated, but also, or more importantly, how they are practised, how they have influenced and shaped the worship patterns of the Indian Church, and to what extent they carry the manyness of the people, the pluriform experiences and expressions of the people, especially of the many subaltern communities.

The Jewish context in which the Christian liturgies originated and the Indian context in which the indigenised liturgies developed were imperial, i.e., within the contexts of the Roman Empire and the British Empire. Bradshaw's "hermeneutics of suspicion" is more relevant in such forms of geopolitical imperialism. However, today, the empire is understood in a broader framework. For Antonio Negri and Michael Hardt, any discourse on empire should not be confused with the medieval and modern military notions about imperialism, but should be understood as a post-globalised human condition where we see the free flow of capital, information and technology, signifying the uneven development of the centre and periphery countries and the irreversible gap between the rich and the poor, and hence, empire has no territorial centre of power and does not rely on any territorial boundaries.

> Empire is materializing before our very eyes. Over the past several decades, as colonial regimes were overthrown and then precipitously after the Soviet barriers to the capitalist world market finally collapsed, we have witnessed an irresistible and irreversible globalization of economic and cultural exchanges. Along with the global market and global circuits of production has emerged a global order, a new logic and structure of rule—in short, a new form of sovereignty. Empire is the political subject that effectively regulates these global exchanges, the sovereign power that governs the world. [...] In contrast to imperialism, Empire establishes no territorial center of power and does not rely on fixed boundaries or barriers. It is a decentered and deterritorializing apparatus of rule that progressively incorporates the entire global realm within its open, expanding frontiers. Empire manages hybrid identities, flexible hierarchies, and plural exchanges through modulating networks of command.

The distinct national colors of the imperialist map of the world have merged and blended in the imperial global rainbow.[32]

According to Kim Young Bok, the emergence of the global empire provides the new global context of theology, a context that is ecumenical and universal, which no theological reflection can overlook, since, "whether one is at the seat and centre of the Empire or at its periphery, one is not outside of the Empire."[33] The only possibility within the empire is to be an alternative to it. For Negri, this alternative is "multitude," "an open and expansive network in which all differences can be expressed freely and equally, a network that provides the means of encounter so that we can work and live in common."[34] Multitude is "many" and hence is different from people that refers to "one," multitude consists of "difference" and hence is different from masses whose essence is "indifference," multitude is "inclusive" and hence is different from the working class that is "exclusive."[35] Thus, multitude as an alternative to the empire,

> [...] is composed of innumerable internal differences that can never be reduced to a unity or a single identity—different cultures, races, ethnicities, genders, and sexual orientations; different forms of labor; different ways of living; different ways of the world; and different desires. The multitude is a multiplicity of all these singular differences.[36]

What Negri and Hardt calls the "multitude", in the Indian context, are the "subalterns" whom Ranajit Guha equates with the "people," the social groups and elements which he designates as the "total Indian population excluding the elites, the dominant groups, foreign and indigenous."[37] The "subaltern" refers to all communities historically, socially, culturally and economically subordinated, those who are oppressed and neglected of the basis of their caste, class, race, religion, gender, sex and age. Bradshaw's "hermeneutics of suspicion," employing the rhizomatic lens, does not appear sufficient enough to deconstruct the liturgical histories and patterns of manyness of/in the subaltern Indian context where empire operates not as a geopolitical entity.

Modes of Liturgical Reimagination in India

In the Indian context, liturgical reimaginations are not new. There have been at least two modes of liturgical reimagination: ecumenical and indigenous (national). There have been several ecumenical reimaginations or representations of liturgies, which of course have enhanced unity between and among diverse church traditions. However, one should not be uncritical of many of those ecumenical reimaginations, as they were initiated merely to safeguard and defend the cause of institutionalised ecclesiastical agendas. Ecumenism, on the one hand, seems to have become a ritual and fashion, practised in order to appear "ecumenical," and on the other hand, appears to have become a strategy or scheme of an alliance, in order to gain or guard power and privileges. In such ecumenical discourses, liturgy is reduced (or degraded) to the role of an agency to reinforce such illegitimate alliances. Often, in ecumenical liturgies, marginality is not represented, except for its decorative role, that too, probably to prove the theological and social commitment of the individual or institution that formulates such liturgies. The point that even the liturgies of two of the united and uniting Churches in India, the Church of South India and the Church of North India, of which the majority of members belong to the marginalised communities, Dalits, Tribals, Adivasis (Adi = original & Vasis = inhabitants) and Fisher People, do not adequately represent their pains and pathos, and hopes and aspirations, validates this fact.

Concerning the indigenous mode of reimagination, through a postcolonial reading of liturgy in India during the colonial and postcolonial period, David Joy exposes several relationships such as those between liturgy and power, liturgy and culture, and liturgy and linguistics, and he establishes that the attempts of indigenisation and Indianisation of liturgy was a mode of resistance.[38] While this is true, one should not be uncritical about those liturgies as well, especially their claim to be "Indian" and representing a "mode of resistance." Regarding the claim to be "Indian," the question is, whose or which India does it represent, and concerning the claim of representing a mode of resistance, the question is whose resistance against whom is represented. In short, the primary challenge for any liturgical reimagination in India, be it ecumenical or national, is how far those types of reimagination represent the manyness of the subaltern voices.

In any colonial/imperial context, the colonised are subalterns—those dominated by the colonised. Hence, any local expressions of inculturation or indigenisation can be considered as a mode of resistance to the colonial. But, in the South Asian contexts, especially in the Indian context, a discourse on subalternity should also consider the issues of caste and gender. Otherwise, such discourses, especially liturgical reimaginations, within the framework of nationalist responses to the colonial forms of worship will remain elitist like the nationalist historiography of India, overlooking the pluriform subaltern experiences.[39] If so, they may fail to realise the ecclesiology "Church as event," never reclaiming their subversive moral agency, and contest the logic and practices of domination, homogenisation and exclusion.[40]

Therefore, in the Indian context, any postcolonial reading of the liturgical field demands a reading through the eyes of subaltern manyness, and hence, it is helpful to juxtapose the "hermeneutics of homework," proposed by Gayatri Chakravorty Spivak, with Bradshaw's "hermeneutics of suspicion," which is yet another attempt for a kind of liturgical reimagination that falls within the postcolonial modes of analysis of empire in which

> [...] social, cultural, religious, gendered, sexual, and economic ways of living are assessed critically by those who have been victimized by patterns of structural domination, and have been dismissed from the historical processes of life creation: namely, the poor, the disenfranchised, the subaltern, the wretched of the earth, and the colonized.[41]

Edward Said to Gayatri Spivak, and "Hermeneutics of Homework": Representing the Manyness of Marginalities

Referring to "Orientalism" as an imperial ideological hegemonic epistemology, Edward Said argues it is not merely a myth or lies or "fantasies," but instead, a construction of theory and practice, an epistemological construction/representation by "the Occident" to retain their political and cultural supremacy over "the Orient" through a relationship of power, of domination, and of varying degrees of a complex hegemony.[42] He observes that in such constructed epistemological representations of "theory and practice," there is an issue of "redispossing" of the representation (or misrepresentation) of the "represented" dominated/colonised by the "representing" dominant and coloniser, whose "representations" are "implicated, intertwined, embedded, interwoven with a great many other things besides 'truth.'"

> [...] the real issue is whether indeed there can be a true representation of anything, or whether any and all representations, because they are representations, are embedded first in the language and then in the culture, institutions and political ambience of the representer. [...] then we must be prepared

to accept the fact that a representation is *eo ipso* implicated, intertwined, embedded, interwoven with a great many other things besides 'truth', which is itself a representation. What this must lead us to methodologically is to view representations (or misrepresentations - the distinction is at best a matter of degree) as inhabiting a common field of play defined for them not by some inherent common subject matter alone, but by some common history, tradition, universe of discourse. Within this field, which no single scholar can create but which each scholar receives and in which he then finds a place for himself, the individual researcher makes his contribution. Such contributions, even for the exceptional genus, are strategies of redisposing material within the field; even the scholar who unearths a once-lost manuscript produces the "found" test in a context already prepared for it, for that is the real meaning of *finding* a new text.[43]

According to Spivak, such representations which are often located within the representers' privileged social locations based on race, class, nationality, gender and the like prevents one from gaining a certain kind of "other knowledge." Therefore, she proposes the "hermeneutics of homework," "a self-reflexive analysis of one's own epistemological and ontological assumptions; in other words, examining how these have been naturalized in and through geopolitical and institutional power relations/practices."[44] While for Bradshaw, his "hermeneutic of suspicion" through the rhizomatic lens enables him to reread the liturgical texts, the "hermeneutics of homework" not only enhances a political reading of the given text (here, liturgical texts), but also helps one to unlearn his/her privilege that marks the beginning of his/her ethical relation with the Other.[45] Further, for Spivak "doing homework is an ongoing practice that includes learning as much as possible about the areas where the hegemony of the dominant and privileged subject is being challenged."[46] Connecting that to her concept of marginality, it challenges the privileged position of centres and the notion that the centre validates the margins, thus marginality becoming a rhetorical and deconstructive domain, moreover where the subaltern becomes the "teacher." Further, this marginality, as she says, is an "irreducible singularity," and hence it offers the logic of manyness that contests the logic of oneness and affirms the diverse experiences and expressions of marginalities in their plurality.

Towards a Subaltern Reimagination of Liturgy: Can the Subaltern Worship?

Rereading the sources of subaltern historiography, employing the "hermeneutic of homework," Spivak concludes that the subaltern cannot speak. Elaborating on Spivak, Y.T. Vinayraj says, "since there is no 'pure'/'uncontaminated' subaltern consciousness devoid of the imprints of the colonizer and thus somebody else must have spoken for him/her."[47] Appropriating the Spivakian logic and incorporating into the discipline of liturgical studies, one could say, since the "imperialist epistemic, social, and disciplinary" representation of subalterns finds itself "inscribed" in the dominant colonial and nationalist elitist liturgies, in which the subalterns leave minimal traces, the subaltern cannot worship.[48] Only through a liturgical reimagination in the Indian context that seriously considers two essential subaltern categories, "chromatism," which refers to race and caste, and "genitalism," which refers to gender, can the subalterns worship.[49]

A subaltern reimagination of liturgy emerges from and expresses subaltern experiences as "contested epistemology," publicly challenging the dominant liturgies of power as expressed through race, caste and gender. Giorgio Agamben says, the term "leitourgia" etymologically signifies "public service," and the

Church has "always tried to underline the public character of liturgical worship in contrast to private devotions."[50] According to Ronald Theimann, the Christian worship is essentially political, the liturgy of the Church extending naturally and directly into political action, as it involves "engaging in public office at one's own expense, thereby offering service to the state and so contribute to the well-being of the community or koinonia."[51] Raj Bharat Patta, elaborating on Agamben and Theimann, asserts that "liturgy served as a public theology of the early church. Such an understanding provides an important rationale in understanding liturgy as a theological account of public."[52] Qualifying the "public" as subaltern public, the real public in contrast to the dominant publics, Patta argues, "Subaltern liturgy of public is liturgy which evolves out of the epistemic experiential sites of subalternity, on the one hand contesting the dominant liturgies of power, and on the other, contesting the public itself, offering 'alternative universalism' as a subaltern public."[53]

A liturgical reimagination through the subaltern representations accentuating the caste, race and gender subaltern experiences and expressions includes "the task of challenging status quo representations and their ideological agenda in reinforcing systems of inequality and subordination."[54] Jagessar and Burns say that to develop such a subaltern reimagination, one should go beyond an act of inculturation, to dislodging dominant and oppressive modes of representing and imaging, and eluding the dominant or status quo proclivity to define and control.

> To dislodge dominant and oppressive modes of representing and imaging demands nothing less. It will mean cultivating and nurturing safe, fluid ecclesial spaces to enable such critical questions by the subaltern communities. This is more than using Nan Bread, wearing colourful Ghanian vestments, covering

the table with multi-coloured cloth or striking a Tibetan gong during our worship. Our (new) metaphors and symbols would challenge any notion of wanting to neatly appropriate differences. They ought to elude the dominant or status quo proclivity to define and control.[55]

The subaltern reimagination of liturgy, incorporating the aspects of manyness and marginality, particularly in the pluralistic and polyphonic South Asian context, calls one to explore the potentials of subaltern liturgies beyond Christendom to realise Church as event ecclesiology. For instance, the "egalitarian, community-centred and people-oriented rituals" in the Dalit liturgies can play a liberative role in reimagining (or reimaging) church as a space of justice and equality.[56] As Abraham Ayrookuzhiyil observes, "There are gods like 'Pottam Teyyam' of the 'Malabar Pulayas' who calls for righteousness and divine retribution.[57] There is a large amount of folk-songs, poems of Dalits and backward classes, saints, who condemn caste, ritualism, pilgrimage, priest-craft and calls for worship of God in spirit and truth."[58] In a similar vein, Sathianathan Clarke in his seminal work, *Dalits and Christianity: Subaltern Religion and Liberation Theology in India*, creatively interprets the "resistive" and the "constructive" dimensions of Dalit rituals by portraying the Dalit drum as a symbolic representation of the Dalits' collective expression and experience of the divine; he interprets Christ as drum.[59] In short, if Church as event ecclesiology needs to become a reality, a subaltern reimagination of liturgies is a compelling call.

With Many Voices: Liturgies in Contexts

This book, *With Many Voices: Liturgies in Contexts*, published as part of the DARE initiative of the CWM South Asian Region, belongs to the series of resource books, entitled 'Reimagining

Church as Event: Perspectives from the Margins.' This particular volume is an attempt to reimagine liturgies and songs that would complement the ecclesiological affirmation of Church as event. It includes experimental liturgies and songs that have emerged out of diverse subaltern contexts. As the name suggests, the aim of this resource book is not to unify diversities, but to acknowledge and affirm diversities, with particular emphasis upon the subaltern domain. It calls for a new epiclesis, where the Holy Spirit descends and dwells not to create "oneness" but rather affirm "manyness." As Ferdinand A. Anno says, such a liturgy, which he calls as "Pentecostal Liturgy," challenges the church to speak languages other than dominant languages and affirm people's insurrection and resurrection, of them breaking free from the hegemonic language and culture of domination.

> A Pentecostal liturgy is hegemony breaking language from and for God. It is a statement of faith that needs reaffirmation in situations where freedom and human rights are curtailed and the church hierarchy maintains its silence and apathy – if not fear—to speak out in public the subversive and 'strange' Word of God.
>
> Moreover, a Pentecostal liturgy of struggle also builds on both the prophecy of Christ and the identity politics of Pentecostals. 'Speaking in tongues' is prophetic speech. It speaks languages other than the dominant one. The languages point to a world other than the present, or 'kingdoms not of this world,' indicting the 'Babel' humanity is building for its self-elevation. On the historical, practical level, 'speaking in tongues' is a lucid, even a literal case of a people's insurrection and resurrection, of a people breaking free from the hegemonic language and culture of domination.[60]

The liturgies included in this book are written by the clergy and the laity, men and women, belonging to diverse church traditions. The liturgies, as well as the songs, address diverse contextual issues such as Dalit, Tribal and Adivasi struggles, cultural nationalism, fascism and globalisation, ecology, womanism and disability, theological education, family and ecumenism. Besides complete version of liturgies, there is also a section for liturgical resources that include several elements of liturgical worship such as confession, affirmation and benediction, subaltern reimaging of Psalms, the Magnificat and the Lord's Prayer, and some directives for symbolic acts. Most of the songs included in this book are set to the tunes of familiar hymns or lyrics.

Conclusion: Colours of Liturgical Reimagination

At the heart of reimagining "Church as event" is the call for a liturgical reimagination. In the Indian context, which is marked by subalternity, such a liturgical reimagination is possible by juxtaposing Bradshaw's "hermeneutics of suspicion" employing the rhizomatic optic and Spivak's "hermeneutics of homework." It is neither the "white" colonial nor the "saffron" nationalist or not even the "rainbow" ecumenical, rather the "kaleidoscopic" subaltern liturgical reimagination that would truly represent the "chromatic" and "genital" subalternities. Such a kaleidoscopic liturgical reimagination by and with the subalterns compels the Church to go beyond her attempts of inculturation/indigenisation, towards uprooting dominant and exploitative forms of representation and challenging the dominant or status quo tendency to define and control. Through such a kaleidoscopic liturgical reimagination, the subalterns can worship.

May I thank God for giving me this opportunity to partner with the Discernment and Radical Engagement (DARE) initiative of the Council for World Mission (CWM). I thank Sudipta Singh, Mission Secretary, Research and Capacity Development, CWM, and George Zachariah, Lecturer, Theological Studies, Trinity Methodist Theological College, Auckland, the Series Editors, for entrusting me with compiling the songs and liturgies composed by eminent theologians and liturgists. My heart goes to all who have contributed to this project. May I also express my gratitude to the ISPCK for consenting to publish this book as a joint publication with the CWM. Most importantly, I thank Colin Cowan for the Foreword, Cláudio Carvalhaes for the Introduction, and Ferdinand Anno for the Afterword. I join with the CWM-DARE team in hoping and praying that this book *With Many Voices: Liturgies in Contexts* would encourage many to explore further the possibilities of ecclesiological reimagination of Church as event, where the sins of classism, racism, casteism and sexism are contested, and thereby to worship God purposefully, fruitfully and meaningfully, liberating and calling people to wholeness.

Endnotes

[1] Margaret Shanthi, 'Worship/Rituals', in *The SCM Dictionary of Third World Theologies*, ed. by Virginia Fabella and Rasiah S Sugirtharajah (London: SCM Press, 2003), 249.

[2] Michael N. Jagessar and Stephen Burns, *Christian Worship: Postcolonial Perspectives* (London and New York: Routledge, 2014), 50.

[3] Paul Avis, 'Introduction to Ecclesiology', in *The Oxford Handbook of Ecclesiology*, ed. by Paul Avis (Oxford: Oxford University Press, 2018), 1–32 (19).

[4] 'Reimagining Church as Event: Perspectives from the Margins' (Council for World Mission, 2019).

[5] George Zachariah, 'Church: A Rainbow Community of Hospitality, Fellowship and Solidarity' <https://www.academia.edu/6774394/Church_A_Rainbow_Community_of_Hospitality_Fellowship_and_Solidarity> [accessed 16 April 2018], 5.

[6] Zachariah, 'Church: A Rainbow Community of Hospitality, Fellowship and Solidarity'.

[7] Zachariah, 'Church: A Rainbow Community of Hospitality, Fellowship and Solidarity'.

[8] Baby Varghese, 'Church as a Worshipping Community: Liturgical Dimensions of Ecclesiology' (presented at the Second International Conference of Ecclesiological Investigations Group, Kottayam: Orthodox Theological Seminary, 2008).

[9] John R. K. Fenwick and Bryan D. Spinks, *Worship in Transition: The Liturgical Movement in the Twentieth Century* (New York: Continuum, 1995), 169.

[10] J. R. Macphail, 'Worship in the Church of South India', *Scottish Journal of Theology*, 17.1 (1964), 25–42 (31).

[11] James Oswald Dykes and others, *The British and Foreign Evangelical Review and Quarterly Record of Christian Literature* (Edinburgh: Johnstone and Hunter, 1854), 126.

[12] Teresa Berger, *Gender Differences and the Making of Liturgical History: Lifting a Veil on Liturgy's Past* (Surrey: Ashgate, 2011), 15-16.

[13] Graham Ward, 'Postmodern Theology', in *The Modern Theologians: An Introduction to Christian Theology since 1918*, ed. by David F. Ford and Rachel Muers, 3rd edn (Massachusetts, Oxford and Victoria: Blackwell Publishing, 2005), 322–38 (322).

[14] Gilles Deleuze and Felix Guattari, *A Thousand Plateaus: Capitalism and Schizophrenia*, trans. by Brian Massumi (Minnesota and London: University of Minnesota Press, 1987), 21.

[15] Teresa Berger, 'Introduction', in *Liturgy in Migration: From the Upper Room to Cyber Space* (Minesota: Liturgical Press, 2012), xi–xxiv (xv).

[16] Berger, *Gender Differences and the Making of Liturgical History: Lifting a Veil on Liturgy's Past*, 16; Paul F. Bradshaw, *The Search for the Origins of Christian Worship: Sources and Methods for the Study of Early Liturgy* (Oxford and New York: Oxford University Press, 2002), 1–20.

[17] Berger, *Gender Differences and the Making of Liturgical History: Lifting a Veil on Liturgy's Past*, 16-17.

[18] The French liturgist, Pierre Lebrun (1661-1729), and the German scholar, Ferdinand Probst (181-1899), many Anglicans and Nonjurors advocated the philological approach.

[19] Bradshaw, *The Search for the Origins of Christian Worship: Sources and Methods for the Study of Early Liturgy*, 5.

[20] Bradshaw, *The Search for the Origins of Christian Worship: Sources and Methods for the Study of Early Liturgy*. 6

[21] Dom Gregory Dix, *The Shape of the Liturgy* (Westminster: Dacre Press, 1945), 48.

[22] Paul F. Bradshaw, 'Continuity and Change in Early Eucharistic Practice: Shifting Scholarly Perspectives', in *Continuity and Change in Christian Worship*, ed. by R. N Swanson (Woodbridge, Suffolk: The Boydell Press, 1999), 1-17 (1).

[23] Bradshaw, *The Search for the Origins of Christian Worship: Sources and Methods for the Study of Early Liturgy*, 7-8.

[24] Robert Taft, 'The Evolution of the Byzantine "Divine Liturgy"', *Orientalia Christiana Periodica*, 43 (1977), 8–30 (8) <https://eparhija-dalmatinska. hr/40E.htm> [accessed 15 October 2017].

[25] Bradshaw, *The Search for the Origins of Christian Worship: Sources and Methods for the Study of Early Liturgy*, 9

[26] Anton Baumstark, *On the Historical Development of Liturgy*, trans. by Fritz West (Minesota: Liturgical Press, 2022), 44.

[27] Bradshaw, *The Search for the Origins of Christian Worship: Sources and Methods for the Study of Early Liturgy*, 12.

[28] Bradshaw, *The Search for the Origins of Christian Worship: Sources and Methods for the Study of Early Liturgy*, 14.

[29] Berger, *Gender Differences and the Making of Liturgical History: Lifting a Veil on Liturgy's Past*, 17.

[30] Bradshaw, *The Search for the Origins of Christian Worship: Sources and Methods for the Study of Early Liturgy*, 17–20.

[31] Daniel G. Van Slyke, 'The Study of Early Christian Worship', in *T & T Clark Companion to Liturgy*, ed. by Alcuin Reid (London: Bloomsbury T & T Clark, 2016), 43–72 (56).

[32] Antonio Negri and Michael Hardt, *Empire* (Cambridge, Massachusetts and London: Harvard University Press, 2000), xi–xiii.

[33] Kim Yong-Bok, 'Asian Quest for Jesus in the Global Empire', *Madang: Journal of Contextual Theology*, 1.2 (2004), 2.

[34] Antonio Negri and Michael Hardt, *Multitude: War and Democracy in the Age of Empire* (New York: Penguin Press, 2004), xiv.

[35] Negri and Hardt, *Multitude: War and Democracy in the Age of Empire.*

[36] Negri and Hardt, *Multitude: War and Democracy in the Age of Empire.*

[37] Ranajit Guha, 'On Some Aspects of the Historiography of Colonial India', in *Subaltern Studies - Volume I: Writings on South Asian History and Society*, ed. by Ranajit Guha (New Delhi: Oxford University Press, 1982), 1–8 (8).

[38] David Joy, 'A Postcolonial Reading of Liturgy in India during the Colonial/Postcolonial Period as a Mode of Resistance', in *Liturgy in Postcolonial Perspectives - Only One Is Holy*, ed. by Claudio Carvalhaes (New York: Palgrave Macmillan, 2015), 189–200 (193).

[39] For details about nationalist historiographies' tendency to be elitist, read Guha, 'On Some Aspects of the Historiography of Colonial India'.

[40] 'Reimagining Church as Event: Perspectives from the Margins'.

[41] Cláudio Carvalhaes, 'Liturgy and Postcolonialism: An Introduction', in *Liturgy in Postcolonial Perspectives - Only One Is Holy*, ed. by Cláudio Carvalhaes (New York: Palgrave Macmillan, 2015), 1–22 (1).

[42] Edward Said, *Orientalism* (Harmondsworth: Penguin, 1985), 5-6.

[43] Edward Said, *Orientalism*.

[44] Juanita Sundberg, 'Decolonizing Posthumanist Geographies', *Cultural Geographies*, 21.1 (2014), 33–47 (39) <https://www.jstor.org/stable/26168540> [accessed 6 March 2018].

[45] Gayatri Chakravorty Spivak, *The Spivak Reader: Selected Works of Gayatri Chakravorty Spivak*, ed. by Donna Landry and Gerald McLean (New York & London: Routledge, 1996), 5.

[46] Rauna Kuokkanen, 'Indigenous Epistemes', in *A Companion to Critical and Cultural Theory*, 321.

[47] Y. T. Vinayaraj, 'Epistemic Shifts in Subaltern Discourse and Methodological Challenges to Christian Theology' (presented at the National Seminar on Methodological Shifts in Indian Christian Theology: A Re-search, Ecumenical Christian Center, Whitefield, Bangalore, 2010), 1.

[48] Gayatri Chakravorty Spivak, 'Can the Subaltern Speak?', in *Marxism and the Interpretation of the Culture*, ed. by Cary Nelson and Lawrence Grossberg (Urbana: University of Illinois Press, 1988), 271–313 (284-285).

[49] Spivak, *The Spivak Reader: Selected Works of Gayatri Chakravorty Spivak*, 4–5.

[50] Giorgio Agamben, *The Kingdom and the Glory: For a Theological Geneology of Economy and Government* (Stanford: Stanford University Press, 2011), 174.

[51] Ronald F. Theimann, *Constructing A Public Theology: The Church in a Pluralistic Culture* (Kentucky: John Knox Press, 1991), 113–14.

[52] Rajbharat Patta, 'Towards a Subaltern Public Theology for India' (University of Manchester, 2018), 170.

[53] Patta, 'Towards a Subaltern Public Theology for India', 177–78.

[54] Jagessar and Burns, 49.

[55] Jagessar and Burns, Christian Worship: Postcolonial Perspectives.

[56] Abraham Ayrookuzhiel, *Essays on Dalits, Religion and Liberation* (Bangalore: CISRS, 2006), 127–28.

[57] The word "Theyyam" emerges from "daivam," meaning god. It is one of the oldest and famous religious ritual dance forms glorifying the goddess. Theyyam dances are always performed by men, they also endorse female roles, wearing interesting make-up and colourful costumes accompanied by several indigenous musical instruments, along with country torches. The main colours used in the make-up are red, yellow and black using only natural cosmetics. The "theyyam" dancers often have headgear made out of coconut leaves and cloth. "Theyyam" and associated "poojas" (rituals) are typically performed in the sacred places, mostly in temples ("Kavus") of goddesses. Themes are centred on the goddess and her exploits and victories over demons.

[58] Ayrookuzhiel, *Essays on Dalits, Religion and Liberation*.

[59] For a detailed reading, see Sathianathan Clarke, *Dalits and Christianity: Subaltern Religion and Liberation Theology in India* (Delhi: Oxford University Press, 1998).

[60] Ferdinand A. Anno, 'Toward a Liturgical Approach to Re-Routing Missions: Resistance Missiology and Liturgics in The Philippine Setting', in *Mission Continues: Global Impulses for the 21st Century*, ed. by Claudia Währisch-Oblau and Fidon Mwombeki (Oxford: Regnum Books International, 2010), 82–91 (88).

Bibliography

Agamben, Giorgio, *The Kingdom and the Glory: For a Theological Geneology of Economy and Government* (Stanford: Stanford University Press, 2011)

Anno, Ferdinand A., 'Toward a Liturgical Approach to Re-Routing Missions: Resistance Missiology and Liturgics in the Philippine Setting', in *Mission Continues: Global Impulses for the 21st Century*, ed. by Claudia Währisch-Oblau and FidonMwombeki (Oxford: Regnum Books International, 2010), 82–91

Avis, Paul, 'Introduction to Ecclesiology', in *The Oxford Handbook of Ecclesiology*, ed. by Paul Avis (Oxford: Oxford University Press, 2018), 1–32

Ayrookuzhiel, Abraham, *Essays on Dalits, Religion and Liberation* (Bangalore: CISRS, 2006)

Baumstark, Anton, *On the Historical Development of Liturgy*, trans. by Fritz West (Minesota: Liturgical Press, 2022)

Berger, Teresa, *Gender Differences and the Making of Liturgical History: Lifting a Veil on Liturgy's Past* (Surrey: Ashgate, 2011)

Bradshaw, Paul F., 'Continuity and Change in Early Eucharistic Practice: Shifting Scholarly Perspectives', in *Continuity and Change in Christian Worship*, ed. by R. N Swanson (Woodbridge, Suffolk: The Boydell Press, 1999), 1–17

———, *The Search for the Origins of Christian Worship: Sources and Methods for the Study of Early Liturgy* (Oxford and New York: Oxford University Press, 2002)

Carvalhaes, Cláudio, 'Liturgy and Postcolonialism: An Introduction', in *Liturgy in Postcolonial Perspectives – Only One Is Holy*, ed. by CláudioCarvalhaes (New York: Palgrave Macmillan, 2015), 1–22

———, Paul Galbreath, and Janet R. Walton, *What's Worship Got to Do with It?: Interpreting Life Liturgically* (Eugene, Oregon: Cascade Books, 2018)

Clarke, Sathianathan, *Dalits and Christianity: Subaltern Religion and Liberation Theology in India* (Delhi: Oxford University Press, 1998)

Deleuze, Gilles, *Difference and Repetition*, trans. by Paul Patton (New York: Columbia University Press, 1994)

Deleuze, Gilles, and Felix Guattari, *A Thousand Plateaus: Capitalism and Schizophrenia*, trans. by Brian Massumi (Minesota and London: University of Minnesota Press, 1987)

Dix, Dom Gregory, *The Shape of the Liturgy* (Westminster: Dacre Press, 1945)

Dykes, James Oswald, James Stuart Candish, Hugh Sinclair Paterson, and Joseph Samuel Exell, *The British and Foreign Evangelical Review and Quarterly Record of Christian Literature* (Edinburgh: Johnstone and Hunter, 1854)

Fenwick, John R. K., and Bryan D. Spinks, *Worship in Transition: The Liturgical Movement in the Twentieth Century* (New York: Continuum, 1995)

Guha, Ranajit, 'On Some Aspects of the Historiography of Colonial India', in *Subaltern Studies - Volume I: Writings on South Asian History and Society*, ed. by Ranajit Guha (New Delhi: Oxford University Press, 1982), 1–8

Jagessar, Michael N., and Stephen Burns, *Christian Worship: Postcolonial Perspectives* (London and New York: Routledge, 2014)

Joy, David, 'A Postcolonial Reading of Liturgy in India during the Colonial/ Postcolonial Period as a Mode of Resistance', in *Liturgy in Postcolonial Perspectives - Only One Is Holy*, ed. by Claudio Carvalhaes (New York: Palgrave Macmillan, 2015), 189–200

Macphail, J. R., 'Worship in the Church of South India', *Scottish Journal of Theology*, 17.1 (1964), 25–42

Negri, Antonio, and Michael Hardt, *Empire* (Cambridge, Massachusetts and London: Harvard University Press, 2000)

———, *Multitude: War and Democracy in the Age of Empire* (New York: Penguin Press, 2004)

O'Donoghue, Neil Xavier, 'The Shape of the History of the Eucharist', *New Blackfriars*, 93.1043 (2012), 71–83

Raj Bharat Patta, 'Towards a Subaltern Public Theology for India' (University of Manchester, 2018)

'Reimagining Church as Event: Perspectives from the Margins' (Council for World Mission, 2019)

Said, Edward, *Orientalism* (Harmondsworth: Penguin, 1985)

Satpathy, Sumanyu, 'Us Not US: Representation and the Pedagogy of Marginality Studies in India', *Indian Literature*, 49.6 (230) (2005), 150–61

Shanthi, Margaret, 'Worship/Rituals', in *The SCM Dictionary of Third World Theologies*, ed. by Virginia Fabella and Rasiah S Sugirtharajah (London: SCM Press, 2003), 249

Slyke, Daniel G. Van, 'The Study of Early Christian Worship', in *T & T Clark Companion to Liturgy*, ed. by Alcuin Reid (London: Bloomsbury T & T Clark, 2016), 43–72

Studiorum, Pontificium Institutum Orientalium, *Comparative Liturgy Fifty Years After Anton Baumstark (1872-1948): Acts of the International Congress, Rome, 25-29 September 1998*, Orientalia Christiana Analecta (Rome: Pontificium Institutum Orientalium Studiorum, 2001)

Sundberg, Juanita, 'Decolonizing Posthumanist Geographies', *Cultural Geographies*, 21.1 (2014), 33–47 <https://www.jstor.org/stable/26168540> [accessed 6 March 2018]

Taft, Robert, 'The Evolution of the Byzantine "Divine Liturgy"', *Orientalia Christiana Periodica*, 43 (1977), 8–30

Theimann, Ronald F., *Constructing A Public Theology: The Church in a Pluralistic Culture* (Kentucky: John Knox Press, 1991)

Varghese, Baby, 'Church as a Worshipping Community: Liturgical Dimensions of Ecclesiology' (presented at the Second International Conference of Ecclesiological Investigations Group, Kottayam: Orthodox Theological Seminary, 2008)

Vinayaraj, Y. T., 'Epistemic Shifts in Subaltern Discourse and Methodological Challenges to Christian Theology' (presented at the National Seminar on Methodological Shifts in Indian Christian Theology: A Re-search, Ecumenical Christian Center, Whitefield, Bangalore, 2010)

Ward, Graham, 'Postmodern Theology', in *The Modern Theologians: An Introduction to Christian Theology since 1918*, ed. by David F. Ford and Rachel Muers, 3rd edn (Massachusetts, Oxford and Victoria: Blackwell Publishing, 2005), 322–38

Yong-Bok, Kim, 'Asian Quest for Jesus in the Global Empire', *Madang: Journal of Contextual Theology*, 1.2 (2004)

Zachariah, George, 'Church: A Rainbow Community of Hospitality, Fellowship and Solidarity' <https://www.academia.edu/6774394/Church_A_Rainbow_Community_of_Hospitality_Fellowship_and_Solidarity> [accessed 16 April 2018]

LITURGIES

1

Farmers' Life:
Hope in the Midst of Injustice[1]

*Santhanam (sandal paste) kept at the entrance is a symbolic welcome of the people into this service. An art, portraying the condition of farmers, and several elements used by them are placed on the altar table. A few minutes before the service, as the **prelude**, a video portraying the struggles of farmers shall be played. The congregation shall watch the video and reflect upon the life of the farmers as they prepare for the worship.*

FARMERS' VOICES

Voice 1: We do not have enough food for our survival. We are dying.

Voice 2: We were forced to pledge our lands and our bodies. Now we don't own both. We are dying.

Voice 3: Is there anyone to help us? Is there anyone who cares about us? We are dying.

---

[1] Liturgy prepared by D. Vetha Prabha Ponraj.

CALL TO WORSHIP

Come and worship God, the Chief Farmer, who plants the flora of the earth.

Come and worship Christ Jesus, the Sower, who sows the seeds on good soil.

Come and worship the Holy Spirit, the Sustainer, who hovers over all creation.

OPENING PRAYER

Gracious God, confronted by the miserable predicament of the farmers, we have gathered in Your presence to listen to Your voice, to be filled by Your Spirit, and to experience Your power. May Your voice unsettle us from the slumber of indifference. May Your Spirit awaken our conscience to discern the miseries of farmers. May Your power empower us to join their struggle for peace and justice. In Jesus' name, we pray, **Amen.**

PRAYER OF PRAISE AND THANKSGIVING

For the sun and rain, soil and seeds, trees and plants,
We thank You, O Lord!

For the rivers and seas, hills and mountains, fields and plains,
We thank You, O Lord!

For the cattle and fowl, milk and egg, fish and meat,
We thank You, O Lord!

For the farmers and their families, their work and labour, their faith and action,
We thank You, O Lord!

FOLK SONG[2] *(Composed in the style of Tamil farmers' traditional song)*

Mathavanga Kuraia Mannikka Sonna Yesu Maga Rasa
Manna Kaakkum Vivasayee Kuraia Kettu Manasu Irangu Rasa
Manneduthu Ellaraium Unnuruvil Padaithavare
Manusanga Usurukkulla Unnusura Koduthavare
Rasa Enga Rasa Kalutha Mela Vantha Rasa
Rasa yesu Rasa Vayakkattila Nadantha Rasa   - Mathavanga

Soru Thantha Samy Avuga Sotthukkaga Yenguranga
Sethu Pona Nilattha Partthu Thanum Saga Thudikkiranga
Vange-ilaKadana Vangi Vakkatthu Poi Nikkuranga
Valkai-ila Thenju Poi Kadanula Saguranga

Unna Vittal Yaru Irukka-2
Enga Kurai a Kekka Yaru Irukka
Enga Kanneer Thudaikka Yaru Irukka   - Mathavanga

Vaanam Partha Bhumithaiyee Navarandu Thavikkaiye-le
Valivarum Kaviriyo Theerpu Vanthum Nanaikkavillai
Nilatthadi Neerai Yellam Coca-Cola Urinjuthu
Nilangalia Madalakki Monsanto Alikkuthu   - Unna Vitta

(Meaning: Jesus, our Lord, who told us to forgive others' mistakes, heed the cry of the farmers who save the soil. You created us from the soil and gave Your life for us. You are the one who walked in fields and lands. The ones who provide food are being deprived of food. At the sight of the dead lands, they want to die. By taking loans from banks, they have become debtors. There is none other than You who can hear and wipe our tears away. The parched lands await water to quench its thirst. The judgment on the

---

[2] Folk song is written by Amos and composed by Kanagaraj.

release of the Cauvery river waters has worsened our woes. The aquifers are depleted by Coca-Cola, and the lands are rendered unproductive by land mafias.)

SCRIPTURE   Nehemiah 5: 1-7; 10-12

VIDEO PRESENTATION *(A video from the Tamil movie* Kathi, *which is a protest against a private company's pillaging of water and land in Thannutthu, a village in Tirunelveli, Tamil Nadu, or a similar video shall be played.)*

HOMILY   Farmers' Life: Hope in the Midst of Injustice

CONFESSION

Wash yourselves; make yourselves clean; remove the evil of your doings from before my eyes; cease to do evil, learn to do good; seek justice. Do not be ashamed to confess your sins.

O God, You have sown the seeds of justice in our heart;

But we have not watered it.

God of the farmers, forgive us.

You have shown us the innocent dying and the wicked prospering;

But we have never responded to Your vision of a just world.

God of justice, forgive us.

You have shown us the poor, the naked, and the homeless wandering without food, clothing and shelter;

But we have never cared for them and only cared for our family and us.

God of the oppressed, forgive us.

ASSURANCE OF PARDON

God is merciful and slow to anger. God has seen your contrite hearts and has forgiven your sins through Jesus, the Christ. Be strong, stand firm and be rooted in the Lord your God to do justice, to love mercy and to walk humbly, **Amen.**

AFFIRMATION OF FAITH (*In unison*)

We believe in God, the creator of life, who made us co-creators and entrusted us to till the ground and make it fruitful.

We believe in Jesus Christ, the Son of God, incarnated as human, resisted all oppressions, was tortured and murdered, resurrected from the dead, who, by His life, death and resurrection, challenges us to participate in God's mission by becoming agents of justice and peace.

We believe in the Spirit of God, who edifies and empowers us to be sensitive to the experiences of debt-ridden farmers, uniting with their struggles for justice and peace.

We believe in the One, Universal Church, and the body of Christ called to become the community of God in bringing social and economic equality and justice. Amen.

INTERCESSORY PRAYERS

Voice 4: My father, Vishal Pawal, is a farmer. He took a loan of Rs. 7 lakh from a bank for the benefit of our land and harvest. But, there being no rain and water, the crops failed for three years. There was no farming, and so we couldn't repay the loan. My father jumped to death in a well. My mother and I wept, saying, "Papa, why did you do this?" In his suicide letter, he wrote that he couldn't make us happy and provide food for us. Now I am responsible for repaying the debt. Is there anyone to pray for the people who are suffering like my family?

Silence

Voice 5: We are the farmers from Tiruchi, Tamil Nadu. We are in the grip of extreme drought due to the failure of the monsoon and non-release of water from the Cauvery river. Owing to crop failure, for five years, we have had no Kuruvai crop, and this year the Samba crop has also failed.[3] So because of the famine, dead rats have become our food. We have given several petitions to the District Collector and also to the Chief Minister. But no one is listening to us. Is there anyone to pray for the people who are in power so that they may listen to the farmers?

Silence

Voice 6: I am Balan from Thanjavur district, Tamil Nadu. I borrowed Rs. 3.80 lakh from a private finance company to buy a tractor. I repaid more than what I owe. So far I have paid Rs. 4.11 lakh. But still, I have to pay two more instalments. When I failed to make the last two payments, I was beaten up by 20 persons, including ten police officers, and my tractor was also taken away. I was beaten in front of my family and the entire village. Is there anyone to pray for the people who drink the blood of the poor?

Silence

Voice 7: I am Asalambal, a farmer from Papanadu, Tanjore district, Tamil Nadu. I have two sons. When my husband died, I had the responsibility to take care of my family and educate my sons. Since there is no water from the Cauvery, we have lost all hope for farming, and there is no rainfall too. My two sons have discontinued their studies and have moved to

---

[3] "Kuruvai" are the crops grown in Cauvery Delta of Tamil Nadu state in India. "Samba Rice" refers to the rice grown in Samba season, i.e., August through January.

neighbouring Telangana to work at a construction site to make a living. We cannot repay the interest on our loan. I have also attempted suicide. Is there anyone to pray for the people who attempt suicide like me?

Silence

Lord, in Your mercy,

Hear our prayers.

THE LORD'S PRAYER *(In our vernacular)*

COMMITMENT SONG[4] *(Set to the tune of "Because He Lives")*

O God, we pray, as we remember
The farmer's life, the farmer's death
Those hands that toil, to fill our hunger
Are now in need, of helping hands, and caring hearts

Chorus   We pledge to care, for the ones who give life
We pledge to work, for their justice
Let's make a world, where farmers live life
With no laments, and injustice, for years to come.

O God, we pray, to strengthen our call
To break our hearts, to feel their pain
Let's raise our voice, and stand for farmers
To offer hope, and dignity, that they deserve   **Chorus**

CLOSING PRAYER

We give You thanks, O God, for strengthening us to worship You in true spirit. Help us, and be with us as we depart from here to carry out the tasks and duties which You have assigned

---

[4] Text by Yajenlemla Chang; Arranged by Arvind Theodore.

to each one of us. May we sow justice, pluck out discrimination and reap the victory of peace and integrity, **Amen.**

BENEDICTION

May God who sows the seeds of integrity, Jesus Christ who waters it with peace and mercy, and the Holy Spirit who helps us to reap justice be with each one of us as we join the farmers and stand for truth and righteousness, now and forever, **Amen.**

2

Ecclesia: (Dis)Figuring (Dis)Ability in the Context[1]

*The members of the community are requested to be **seated throughout the worship** to experience and participate in the worship as many with disabilities do.*

PRELUDE

As we listen to the prelude, let us prepare our minds and hearts for worship.

VOICES OF PEOPLE LIVING WITH/IN THE CONTEXT OF DISABILITIES

Voice 1: We are created in God's image, but we are seen as a cause of disgrace and punishment.

Voice 2: We are forced to be the recipients of discrimination in all forms. We are not even considered as worthy human lives.

---

[1] Liturgy prepared by Bijin John Varghese.

Voice 3: Many a time, we become objects of charity rather than subjects of inclusivity.

CALL TO WORSHIP

Come and worship God, the Creator who creates all human beings in the divine image.

Come and worship Jesus Christ, the Liberator who liberates people from their weaknesses.

Come and worship the Holy Spirit, the Sustainer who sustains hope among the broken people.

OPENING PRAYER (*In Unison*)

Gracious and loving God, we thank You for Your presence this day as we gather together as a community of believers. Unsettle and disturb us as we pray for people with disabilities in our society, especially those who have become objects of our prejudices, judgement and 'other'ness. Strengthen and help us to (dis)figure the inhibited perceptions of disability so that we live in mutual love and acceptance. In Jesus' name, we pray, **Amen.**

PRAISE AND THANKSGIVING

For people like Helen Keller, Albert Einstein, Ludwig van Beethoven, Stephen Hawking, Nick Vujicic, Sudha Chandran, Arunima Sinha, Preethi Srinivasan and many others who despite their (dis)abilities have contributed generously to the society at large.

We praise and thank You, Lord.

For theologians like Nancy Eiesland, Amos Yong, Deborah Beth Creamer, K.C. Abraham, for their thoughts and contributions to (dis)figure the notions of a transcendent God.

We praise and thank You, Lord.

For organisations like Ecumenical Disability Advocates Network (EDAN), Association of People with Disability (APD), Liza's Home, Provision Asia and many others for their self-effacing contributions in the lives of people with disabilities.

We praise and thank You, Lord.

MALAYALAM BHAJAN[2]

Angabhangnaya Aruma Nadha

Ashaktharkayi Adiyettone

Avaniyil Angaheenaram Njagalil

Ashvasam Aalambam Angu Mathram

> Yeshu Nadha Sreeyeshunadha
>
> Sharanam Sharanam Sreeyeshunadha
>
> Shayana Kidakkayil Shayadhamekathe
>
> Sharanikaattidu Sharanyam Nalkidu

Angabhangaril Angaye Kaanuvaan

Angapalakaen Mizhikal Thurakkane

Angayin Sathyashishyaray Theerneedan

Achanjala Sevayekan Bhalamekane. (YeshuNadha…)

(Meaning: Loving Lord, on earth, for the weak, disfigured and hurt in the flesh, You alone are the solace and support. Lord Jesus, You are our support when illness confines us to bed. Lord, have mercy, and grant us Your strength. Our Protector, open our eyes to see You in the deformed, so that we become Your faithful disciples, strengthened to consistently serve You.)

---

[2] Text by Jose R. Chennerkara; Music by Lobin Linesh

| **SCRIPTURE READING** | Acts of the Apostles 3: 1-8 |
| **HOMILY** | Ecclesia: (Dis)figuring (Dis)ability in the Context |

CALL TO CONFESSION

Many a time we rely on our thoughts and prejudices for the dissemination of justice to the needy. Today, let us pause for a moment and listen to the feeble disregarded voices of people with disabilities. Let us draw near to God and confess our sins together.

CONFESSION OF SIN (*In unison*)

"Disabled" God, we confess that we have sinned against You and the people with disabilities and others in terms of our social, theological and ecclesial notions about a perfect figure. Even though we have contributed generously to their lives, we tend to see them as the "other." We have often looked, perceived and objectified people with disabilities, sympathising their predicament instead of empathising with their feelings and needs. We beseech Your pardon and forgiveness. We pray that You renew our (dis)figured notions about human perfection, so that we commit ourselves to embrace the "other" in our thoughts, actions and discourses. Amen.

ACT OF CONFESSION

Members representing the worshipping community are requested to enter the altar and tear off the biblical, social and ethical channels of discrimination and embrace those (dis)figured faces to an ecclesial inclusivity.

ASSURANCE OF PARDON

Sisters and Brothers, "disabled" God is always merciful and slow to anger. God has seen your act of confession and has forgiven your sins through Jesus, the disabled Christ. Be conscious of your act and resemble that action through (dis)figuring the "abled" paradigm of perceptions within us that sets you free.
We are free, indeed. Amen.

AFFIRMATION OF FAITH *(In unison)*

We believe in "disabled" God, the creator of everything that proclaims the image of God in the diversity of creation.

We believe in Jesus, the "disabled" Christ who transgresses the "able-bodied" eternal God by taking over human limitations, weaknesses and (dis)abilities in multiple respects through the process of "enfleshment" and was also indicted and smitten on a par with people with disabilities and bore the marks of (dis)ability.

We believe in the Spirit of God, who strengthens and embodies hope in the lives of people with disabilities and gives us the discernment to identify the (dis)abilities within us and not to be prejudiced over our completeness, perfection and wholeness.

We believe in one, an inclusive Church of all and for all, and the body of Christ that breaks and transforms the demarcating and discriminatory laws of purity and pollution and envisions itself as an "abled Church."

INTERCESSORY PRAYER[3]

Voice 4: I am Aashitha from the district of Kasaragod, Kerala. I became blind in the early days of my childhood. My brother was born with intellectual disabilities. During my childhood days, I heard the sound of helicopters used for aerial spraying of Endosulfan and we the children of the village would go out to see it. But we were not sure at that time that they were taking our lives.

Voice 5: I am Rakesh, a migrant daily labourer at Bangalore, hailing from Assam. My seven-year-old son had a crippled leg from birth. My wife and I have taken him to different hospitals to get him proper treatment. For his schooling, we tried to enrol him in a nearby special school. But the authorities are asking for my ID, salary sheet and local address proof. I don't have any. What should I do?

Voice 6: We belong to a prominent Christian denomination in Hosur, Bangalore. Our daughter has been identified with Down's syndrome since her birth. Our Church helps us financially to an extent. The intense gaze of our fellow Churchgoers when my child expressed herself during worships made us feel excluded and as an object of charity by the Church.

Let us spend a few moments in silence, remembering them and many others like them.

Silence

Lord in Your mercy,
Hear our prayers.

---

[3] Names changed.

THE LORD'S PRAYER *(In the language of your hearts)*

COMMITMENT SONG[4] *(Set to the tune of the Hymn "I'm not ashamed to own...")*

> Crippled from birth, without a worth
> This lame laid down with pain
> Neither silver nor any wealth,
> But Jesus, did he gain.
>
> > Help us see them as not objects of charity
> > Carve us that we be your instrument
> > Of your kindness, love and empathy,
> > The channels of your endless bliss.
>
> T'was on our 'ccount, He bore those wounds,
> Disabled by our sin,
> Reconciled us, we may not doom,
> Be abled as his kin.
>
> > At the cross, at the cross, where he was indicted,
> > There the burden of our hearts rolled away,
> > It was there by our faith, judged us pardoned,
> > And now we are happy all the day!

ACT OF COMMITMENT

As the commitment song is sung, the members of the worshipping community are requested to pull down the papers that resemble figured attitudes, discrimination, programmes and ventures of disability and make the tree of perfection visible in its true created form and beauty.

---

[4] Text by Bino Jacob; Music by R.E. Hudson. The song is set to the tune of the hymn "I'm not ashamed to own," by Isaac Watts.

CLOSING PRAYER

"Disabled" God, we thank You for Your presence through which we were enabled to identify and recognise our mistaken perceptions of purity, beauty, wholeness and completeness. Strengthen us not to build beautiful gates through our actions and deeds. May we depart from here (dis)figured, challenged and disturbed so that we become agents of change in our Church and in society. **Amen**

BENEDICTION

May the God Almighty who became "disabled", Jesus the "disabled" Christ who bore the marks of disability and the Holy Spirit who helps people with disabilities be with each one of us to (dis)figure society and the ecclesia to be inclusive for now and forever.

Amen *(Threefold)*

POSTSCRIPT

Although this liturgy is printed in black on a white paper in this book, originally this liturgy was published on sky-blue paper. The sky-blue colour signifies freedom, expression, compassion and acceptance of people with disabilities in the community. All the 'Voices' were printed in red colour to represent the pain and cry of people with disabilities.

The 'Tree of Perfection' during the worship signifies our mistaken attitudes, programmes and ventures for people with disabilities by the society and the Church, that often discriminate them.

3

Family:
Within and Beyond Blood Relation[1]

PRELUDE

During the prelude, let us prepare ourselves for worship. All the congregation members are requested to be seated as families.

CALL TO WORSHIP

Come,

Let us worship God who created and blessed the first family at the Garden of Eden.

Let us exalt Jesus Christ who embraced and called everyone around him as His mother, brother and sister.

Let us discern the guidance of the Holy Spirit in our family.

---

[1] Liturgy prepared by Samuel Ragland Paul.

OPENING PRAYER

God of all families, we come before You with heartfelt gratitude for the gift of family that You have bestowed on us. Help us to celebrate this special gift with thankfulness and with a humble heart. Give us the strength to reach people beyond our families and accept them as members of our family just as Christ did. Inspire and mould us to do Your will. We ask this in the name of our Lord and Saviour, Jesus Christ, **Amen.**

OPENING HYMN[2]   Praise, My Soul, the King of Heaven

RESPONSIVE READING   Psalm 127 & Psalm 128

LITANY OF THANKSGIVING

Grandparents: For guiding us in our long journey of life and for granting Your strength to us in this old age. Indeed, we are privileged to see our children's children.

We thank You, O God.

Parents: For blessing us with wonderful children. We are grateful for the understanding and love we have between our kids and us.

We thank You, O God.

Children: For giving us such caring and loving mother and father who would do anything for our happiness. For the things they do for us even at the cost of their work and priorities.

We thank You, O God.

---

[2] Text by Henry Francis Lyte (1834); Tune: Lauda Anima, composed by John Goss

All: **For the company of each other in times of joy and sorrow, better and worse, sickness and health, fun and play, sharing and encouraging, we thank You, O God. For the people who made our lives happy, made us smile, we thank You. Even though they were not part of our family, they all made a lasting impression in our hearts and lives by their love.**

SCRIPTURE READINGS

Old Testament	Genesis 1: 26-30
Epistle	Ephesians 6: 1-4
Gospel	Saint Mark 3: 31-35
HYMN	Our Parent, by Whose Name[3]
SERMON	Family: Within and Beyond Blood Relation

CONFESSION

Couples: We admit that at times we have not been considerate and understanding to our spouse and our children. At times we have fought and hurt each other over small issues by our words and actions. Sometimes we have been adamant with our own list without considering the views and opinions of our partners. We plead that You have mercy on us and give us a fresh beginning.

Parents: We confess that at times we have not been kind and loving towards our kids. We have failed to

---

[3] By F. Bland Tucker

appreciate their talents and creativity and have often compared them with other kids. Help us to understand that You have wonderfully created our kids. At times, we have forced our kids to do and choose what we wanted them to do or study, but have not considered what their choices were. Moreover, often we have not been considerate to our aged parents. Make us remember the hardships they had gone through to bring us up and to realise that it is our responsibility to take care of them with much love and care.

Teenagers: We confess that many a time we have despised the pieces of advice given to us by our parents, elders and teachers. We had often liked to do what we desired even as we knew that we were not doing right. We have sometimes disobeyed our parents and hurt them. Make us realise that they advise for our best and have our safety in mind.

Children: Jesus, we know that we have been naughty and mischievous, often giving trouble to our parents. Many a time we do not listen to them and do things they tell us not to do. We have often been adamant and stubborn to get what we want by throwing tantrums, crying or refusing to eat food. Jesus, forgive us and help us to be obedient to our parents.

All: *(Holding each other's hands)*

We, as a family, confess, O God, that we have always identified our family through our blood relation. We have failed in reaching out to people and friends who are destitute and homeless, orphans, widows, childless, and who are in need. Make us realise that family isn't always blood. It is the people in our lives who want us in theirs, the ones who accept us for who we are, the ones who long for a family like we have, the ones who long for the love of a mother, father, brother or sister, the ones who would do anything to see us smile and who love us no matter what. In Jesus' name we pray, Amen.

ABSOLUTION

Our God is most merciful, abounding in Grace and His unfailing love endures forever. Thus, take heart and live in confidence because God has forgiven our families and us through His Son Jesus Christ in whom the old is gone and the new has come.

God, we thank You for Your unfailing love and mercy. Praise be to You now and forever.

AFFIRMATION OF FAITH[4]

We believe in God, the one who created and blessed the family of Adam and Eve and our ancestors so that they may have fellowship with You and experience Your providence, love and care.

We believe in Jesus Christ, who was born into a family to a loving couple; who was cared, fed, clothed, disciplined and brought up in fear of God by His parents; who was a responsible brother to His siblings and who cared for His mother even at the cross; who accepted people beyond His

---

[4] Modified

family members and addressed His listeners as mother and siblings thus breaking the notion of family solely based on blood relations.

We believe in the Holy Spirit, who is our guide and who accompanies us in our family journey, challenges us and prompts us to help people who are in need and invites us to accept them as members of our family.

We believe in the Church, which is the universal family of God and is open to all who need a family and who want to experience the tender love and care of the family.

We believe and hope for Your kingdom to come, in which there will not be anyone homeless, orphans, widows and destitute, but a family of all rejoicing in You and experiencing the presence of each other.

INTERCESSORY PRAYERS

Gracious God, we pray for those who have made our life happy. Bless them and help us to make their life happy too. We pray for the people who long to belong to a family. O God, challenge us to reach such people and accept them as members of our family. **Lord, be gracious unto us and hear our prayers.**

We pray for those families in conflict and couples who are not in good terms due to several reasons, that You bring peace and a sense of understanding in such families. We pray for children who long for their parents to spend time with them that Your Spirit would inspire their parents to realise that their kids want their company. We pray for all couples who are expecting the gift of a child, pregnant women waiting for safe delivery, parents who are wishing a good future of their kids. **Lord, be gracious unto us and hear our prayers.**

We pray for the families who have lost their dear ones. God, grant them peace and hope. Also, we remember all people who are away from their families due to work and studies. May Your presence be with them and let them experience Your presence and guidance.

Lord, be gracious unto us and hear our prayers.

Let us all pray the Lord's Prayer together.

Our Father in heaven, hallowed be Your Name, Your Kingdom come, Your will be done on earth as it is in heaven. Give us today our daily bread and forgive us our sins as we forgive those who sin against us. Lead us not into temptation but deliver us from evil. For, Yours is the kingdom, the power and the glory forever and ever. Amen.

OFFERTORY HYMN[5]   O Lord, May Church and Home Combine

CLOSING PRAYER

God, we thank You for binding us together with Your presence in this worship. Thank You for helping us to celebrate and take part in this worship with our family. As we depart from this place as one family to reach out to various people in this world to invite them into ours, we ask for Your strength and presence to go before us. Continue to be with our families and give us the courage and unity to face our problems and hardships as one family, helping and encouraging each other. We ask all this in the name of the One who gives us the courage and strength to stand firm in our commitment, Jesus Christ our Lord. **Amen.**

---

[5] By Carlton C. Buck (1961)

COMMISSION & BENEDICTION

Go into the world with joy and hope and recognise the people whom you come across as a father, mother, sister or brother to you. Transform this world into one family with the love of our Lord and Saviour Jesus Christ, the blessing of God and the guidance of the Holy Spirit continuing to be with us now and forever. **Amen.**

CLOSING HYMN[6]   Blest be the Tie that Binds

---

[6] Text by John Fawcett (1782); Tune: Dennis, composed by Hans Georg Nägeli.

4

Bread and Wine as Channels of Life[1]

INTRODUCTORY SENTENCES
Look:

> The toads are peeping
> in every single marsh,
> and everywhere above me,
> flocks of birds are singing
> with their rousing voices.
> And so the rains have started.
>
> Because of it, my large eyes
> have begun to water,
> for his chariot has not yet begun
> to move an inch in my direction.
>
> - Ainkurunuru 453, trans. Martha Ann Selby,
The Circle of Six Seasons

---

[1] *Liturgy prepared by J. Jayakiran Sebastian.*

OPENING HYMN[2] *(Set to the tune of "Hymn to Joy")*

Come and find the quiet centre
In the crowded life we lead,
Find the room for hope to enter,
Find the frame where we are freed:
Clear the chaos and the clutter,
Clear our eyes that we can see
All the things that really matter,
Be at peace, and simply be.

Silence is a friend who claims us,
Cools the heat and slows the pace,
God it is who speaks and names us,
Knows our being, touches base,
Making space within our thinking,
Lifting shades to show the sun,
Raising courage when we're shrinking,
Finding scope for faith begun.

In the Spirit let us travel,
Open to each other's pain,
Let our loves and fears unravel,
Celebrate the space we gain:
There's a place for deepest dreaming,
There's a time for heart to care,
In the Spirit's lively scheming
There is always room to spare.

---

[2] Text by Shirley Erena Murray; Tune of *Hymn to Joy* (8.7.8.7.D)

PRAYER OF THANKSGIVING

O Lord our God, giving thanks seems so simple and yet calls forth so much from us. Saying thanks for all that You have been, all that You are, and all that we hope You will be for us is the easy part. What is not so simple is to recognise that giving thanks has consequences—consequences in terms of understanding who it is that we are, why we are the way we are, and what we can do to become what You want us to be.

In giving thanks for the ordinariness of our lives, we acknowledge that You call us to recognise that in the ordinary is the potential for the extraordinary and that we are ordinary people whom You call to make extraordinary claims, and for this we are thankful.

In giving thanks for the fragmentation of our lives, we recognise that You fill all our lives with the awareness of the reality that you work to fit the fragments into your perfect completeness.

In giving thanks for our place in the world, and for the ways in which Your world impacts our lives, we thank You for the wonder and the dread that this arouses in us, wonder at our insignificance and dread because of the infinity of space and time.

In the midst of our anxieties and fears, we give You thanks that You know who we are, and that You call us by name to be Yours, just as You offer Yourself to us.

Make our act of thanksgiving truly meaningful and may our lives reflect, to some extent, the reality of what it means to be truly thankful.

This we pray in and through the one whose very life was lived in thankfulness to You, Jesus our Christ and our Lord. **Amen.**

ACT OF REPENTANCE

Having given thanks let us spend some time, examining ourselves and presenting ourselves to the one who is not deceived by the masks that we wear, but who examines our hearts.

Silence

Let us acknowledge before God that we are sorry for certain things that we have done, and sorry for those things that we have left undone.

Silence

Let us acknowledge before God the many occasions we have not allowed the water of life to flow through the channels that God has made, but have obstructed the flow, especially when we thought that others would benefit.

Silence

Let us acknowledge before God that we have drowned the still small voice because we raised our voices in order to have the last word.

Silence

WORDS OF ASSURANCE

If we are truly contrite, our God is one who welcomes us, and offers us the chance of living a renewed and transformed life. This is the good news, that God sets us free from the burdens of the past to become God's children once again. This is our faith that leads to the hope that we can truly love God and one another in ways that bring about healing and reconciliation. **Amen.**

SCRIPTURE READING

Lesson 1   Exodus 24: 3-11

Collect[3]

Festive Father, You created us hungry. We must eat to live. And eating is a necessary habit, a wonderful reminder that we are, after all, creatures. But even more wonderful, You gave us Your Son to be the host of the great meal, the glorious celebration of Your peaceable kingdom. It is a meal of pain. It is a meal of unbounded joy. In our eating, You story us. Give our eating purpose, make us participants in Your unending sacrifice for all your creation. Thank You for making us hungry. May we eat in peace. **Amen.**

Lesson 2   I Corinthians 11: 23 -33

SPECIAL SONG

SERMON   Bread and Wine as Channels of Life

INTERCESSORY PRAYERS

CLOSING PRAYER[4]

May God,

Who clothes the flowers

Who feeds the birds of the sky

Who leads the lambs to pasture

And the deer to water,

Who multiplied loaves and fishes

And changed water into wine

Lead us

Feed us

---

[3] Stanley Hauerwas, "Thank you for making us hungry," in *Prayers Plainly Said* (Downers Grove: InterVarsity Press, 1999), p. 101.

[4] Celtic Blessing (adapted).

Keep us
And change us
Until we reflect
The glory of our Creator
Through all eternity. **Amen.**

COMMUNION HYMN[5]

Time now to gather, time now to feel
Christ's holy presence gracing this meal
Grain from the harvest, fruit of the vine;
Simple the supper, sacred the sign.

Time to remember Christ who was sent.
Time to say, "Thank you" for all he meant.
Come to this table. Come, without fear.
God will forgive you, welcome you here.

All who are hungry, come, and be fed.
Serve one another this cup and bread.
All who are troubled, hurting, or sad,
Come, and find healing. Come, and be glad!

COMMUNION PRAYERS

Beloved in Christ, the good news testified to in the Gospels remind us how Jesus was raised from death and appeared to Mary Magdalene, and also that He sat at table with bewildered disciples and was made known to them in the breaking of the bread. And now as we prepare this table here and now, at this

---

[5] Text by Mary Nelson Keithahn, to be sung in the tune of "Have Thine Own Way Lord" (5.4.5.4.D).

time in this place, we remind ourselves that the table is prepared for all those who wish to experience the presence of the risen Christ and to share in the community of all God's people.

This is truly a joyful feast of the people of God. Women and men, youth and children, come from east and west, north and south, and various directions in-between, and gather at the table of the Lord.

The Lord be with you

And also with you

Let us give thanks to the Lord our God

It is appropriate to offer God thanks and praise

We give You thanks, God of love and God of glory, for calling forth creation and for raising us to life through the breath of Your being.

We thank You for the beauty and bounty of the earth, the fruit of Your creation and the fruit of human labour, and we look forward to that day when sharing by all will mean scarcity to none.

We give You thanks for our ancestors in faith and we thank You for the many examples of lives well lived which we can emulate.

We rejoice that You call the human family to this table of sacrifice and victory. We come in remembrance and celebration of the gift of Jesus, whom You sent in the fullness of time to not only proclaim the good news but to incarnate the good news. We also give You thanks for his death that teaches us how to live in Christ and how to die in Christ.

Send down, O God, the one who pleads for us, the Spirit of love and reconciliation, who seeks to remind us of what Jesus said and about who He was and is and strives to unfold our hearts and minds to recognise and respond to truth. May this Spirit quicken us and bless us and these gifts that are so freely given. With Your daughters and sons of faith in all places throughout the ages, we join the powers of heaven and praise you with joy, saying,

Holy, holy, holy God of love and splendour, the whole universe reflects Your glory. Blessed is the one who comes in the name of our God and embraces those who are excluded. Hosanna in the highest.

Merciful God, as sisters and brothers in faith, we recall anew these words and acts of Jesus, who took bread, blessed it, broke it and gave it to the disciples saying: "Take, eat, this is my body." In like manner, Jesus took a cup, and having given thanks, gave it to the disciples, saying: "Drink it, all of you; for this is my blood of the new testament, which is poured out for many for the forgiveness of sins."

We remember His words that He would not drink again of the fruit of the vine until the heavenly banquet where He would drink it anew when God's reign is truly manifest, and proclaim with courage and faith,

Christ's death, O God, we proclaim
Christ's resurrection, O God, we declare
Christ's coming again, O God, we await.
Glory be to You, O God.

Come, Holy Spirit, come. Bless this bread and bless this wine. Bless all of us as we eat and drink at this table and open our eyes and our hearts that we may recognise the presence of the risen Christ in our midst, in each other, and in all for whom Christ lived and in all for whom Christ died. **Amen.**

Sharing of the Bread and Wine

PRAYER OF THANKSGIVING

Having partaken in the gift of Christ's body and blood, let us give thanks, saying:

Almighty God, we give You thanks for the simplicity and majesty of this meal and for the gift of our Saviour's presence in and through it. Unite us with all who continue to be fed by Christ's body and blood, and use us to continue to faithfully proclaim the good news in this world of chaos and uncertainty, so that we can point to the rainbow of hope and promise, even while the waters of turmoil and confusion rise all around us. **Amen.**

BENEDICTION

May grace beyond our every measure, grace beyond our calculation, grace beyond our human scheming be ours. May grace abundant be ours to experience and acknowledge. Encircled by this grace today and always may we depart from here acknowledging the goodness of our God, Creator, Redeemer, and Enabler, the God of all grace. **Amen.**

CLOSING HYMN[6]

Brother, sister, let me serve you,
let me be as Christ to you;

---

[6] Text by Richard Guillard, [from *Common Ground: A Song Book for all the Churches* (Edinburgh: St. Andrew Press, 1998), No. 16]; Tune: Stuttgart (8.7.8.7.) composed by (attributed to) Christian Friedrich Witt.

pray that I may have the grace to
let you be my servant too.

We are pilgrims on a journey,
and companions on the road;
we are here to help each other
walk the mile and bear the load.

I will hold the Christ-light for you
in the night-time of your fear;
I will hold my hand out for you,
speak the peace you long to hear.

I will weep when you are weeping
when you laugh I'll laugh with you;
I will share your joy and sorrow
till we've seen this journey through.

When we sing to God in heaven
we shall find such harmony,
born of all we've known together
of Christ's love and agony.

Brother, sister, let me serve you,
let me be as Christ to you;
pray that I may have the grace to
let you be my servant too.

5

Discerning the Special[1]

OPENING PRAYER

Dear God, we thank You for bringing us together today at this time in this place to offer You our service of praise and thanksgiving. Help us to value what is truly valuable. Help us to put aside the things that we have set up as idols, diverting us from our calling and our commitment to the values of love, hope and faith. We recognise that we have disguised these idols and clothed them with what we hold to be valuable to us. Grant us the power of discernment to unveil these idols and recognise them for what they are. Thank You for promising us that even though the powers and values of the world and the attractiveness of doing evil seduce us with their promises, in and through the example of Jesus, we have a model that we can emulate. In His death on the cross we recognise the simultaneous humiliation of the child of God and the exaltation of the human one. May Your spirit help us to continue to confess Him as "Lord" and

---

[1] *Liturgy prepared by J. Jayakiran Sebastian.*

persist in leading us into new truth, reminding us of the values for which He lived and for which He died. **Amen.**

HYMN[2]   Called as Partners in Christ's Service

Called as partners in Christ's service,
Called to ministries of grace,
We respond with deep commitment
Fresh new lines of faith to trace.
May we learn the art of sharing,
Side by side and friend with friend,
Equal partners in our caring
To fulfil God's chosen end.

Christ's example, Christ's inspiring,
Christ's clear call to work and worth,
Let us follow, never faltering,
Reconciling folk on earth.
Men and women, richer, poorer,
All God's people, young and old,
Blending human skills together
Gracious gifts from God unfold.

Thus new patterns for Christ's mission,
In a small or global sense,
Help us bear each other's burdens,
Breaking down each wall or fence.
Words of comfort, words of vision,

---

[2] Text by Jane Parker Huber (1981), Tune: Beecher, composed by John Zundel (8.7.8.7 D)

Words of challenge, said with care,
Bring new power and strength for action,
Make us colleagues, free and fair.

So God grant us for tomorrow
Ways to order human life
That surround each person's sorrow
With a calm that conquers strife.
Make us partners in our living,
Our compassion to increase,
Messengers of faith, thus giving
Hope and confidence and peace.

PRAYER OF CONFESSION[3]

O Lord our God, in this theological community forgive us from

- reading without fervour

- speculation without devotion

- investigation without admiration

- observation without exaltation

- industry without piety

- knowledge without love

- understanding without humility

- study without divine grace

Our eternal and interacting God, we recognise and confess that we have failed to respond adequately to Your gracious and

---

[3] Adapted from *The Journey of the Mind Toward God* by Bonaventure (1221–1274)

indwelling presence in our lives. Through Jesus You have offered us new possibilities of living fulfilled and enriched lives along with the freedom to serve you. We confess that we continue to be captives to envy and that pride fills us with a sense of arrogance and self-sufficiency. The wrong that we do is made worse by the good that we do not do. Forgive us we pray and reconcile us to you and to all people. We humbly affirm that You do not put us to shame, but deal wondrously with us, restoring us to health and wholeness.

God of mercy, forgive us and strengthen us to live our life as you intend it. This we pray through Jesus, the One who understands us, knows us, and yet welcomes us. **Amen.**

SCRIPTURE READING

Reading 1　　　　　Song of Songs 5: 9-16

Special Song

Reading 2　　　　　Saint John 1: 43-46

PRAYERS FOR ALL PEOPLE

Let us pray that the nations of the world will follow the path of understanding, peace and concord, and make it possible that all their citizens lead a life of dignity.

Hear us, good Lord.

Grant us abundant harvests, save us from famine and drought, and help us to conserve the richness of the earth and use earth's resources well.

Hear us, good Lord.

May Your Spirit enliven, illumine and enlighten all who teach and all who learn, and reveal to them Your leading in their lives.

Hear us, good Lord.

Save all those who are in danger and protect those who are in trouble; be with those who travel by land, air, or water; show pity and mercy on those who are held captive.

Hear us, good Lord.

Strengthen all women and men, especially those who are maligned or abused, misunderstood or persecuted for what they are or for what they stand for; protect all young children, especially those who are unloved and unwanted; assure the aged with the gift of Your presence, especially those languishing in situations where the love of their families is absent.

Hear us, good Lord.

Shield those who have lost their spouses, the orphaned, those who have fled their homeland, those who are homeless, unemployed, and those who feel lonely and lost, alienated and forgotten.

Hear us, good Lord.

Heal those who are sick in body or tormented in mind, give skill and compassion to all those who care for them, guide those who research the causes of illness and those who probe the mysteries of the human body.

Hear us, good Lord.

SILENT PRAYER

SERMON   Seeing the Speciality

CLOSING HYMN[4]

Moving on from prayer and praise
From being challenged by Your word
In your presence keep us safe

---

[4] Text by J. Jayakiran Sebastian (2004), set to the tune of *Savannah* (7.7.7.7), composed by Johannes Thommen.

Make us instruments of grace.

From delusions of grandeur
From self-pride and arrogance
Thinking that we hold the key
Move us to humility.

How can we respond to You?
Translating the message now
Thought and action interlinked
How and where and why and what?

Questions linger, targets fade
That which was will ever be
Lapsing into compromise
Life goes on, no change we see.

Satisfied by what exists
Playing the game for all to see
Lip-sympathy, easy words
Fleeing forth from commitment!

Don't we have our life to lead?
Idealism — what is that?
What's at stake is survival
Find and hold the middle ground.

We who keep our eyes wide shut
Can't perceive the crying need
Opportunities pass by
Undisturbed we fail again.

"Come and see" — the call goes forth
What is it that we can see?
Unremarkable, despised,
Is he all there is to see?

From appearance to the fact
From the surface to the depth
We respond with joy and hope
Good news active here and now.

BENEDICTION[5]

May everything in us be blessed;
And may we bless every one
And everything.
May we be bathed in the blessings
That the Great Blesser
Delights to shower upon us.
May we be saved from the sourness
That corrodes the person
Who neglects to bless.
May we be used to bring forth buds of hope
Bring fruitfulness to this stagnant earth
May flowers and beauty bloom on it
May friendship grow on it
May songs burst forth
And dancing, loving, creating

---

[5] From *Celtic Blessings: Prayers for Everyday Life* (Chicago: Loyola Press, 1999), pp. 157–158.

After sluggish, barren years.
The blessing of God and the Lord be ours,
The blessing of the perfect Spirit be ours,
The blessing of the Three be pouring on us
Mildly and generously, more and more
Now and forever. **Amen.**

———————

6

The Gospel in a Groaning World
An Ecumenical Liturgy[1]

CALL TO WORSHIP

Sisters and brothers in Christ, we as a community are called to publicly witness our God, our Parent, Caregiver and Sustainer by worshipping together. Come, let us worship God who groans with all, who groans for all and through the groans manifests the gospel.

BHAJAN

Hei Baghvan Tarunam

Sambalatho Ragu Saheletham

Gagane Pavane, Vana UpaVanane

Kala, Kala Jarane Tarunam

---

[1] *This liturgy, prepared by R. Christopher Rajkumar, was originally used during the Inaugural Worship Service of the 27th Quadrennial Assembly of the National Council of Churches in India. The liturgy published here is a modified version.*

A JOYFUL COMMUNITY RESPONSE (Psalm 100)

Make a joyful noise to the Lord, all the lands!

Saranam, Saranam, Saranam[2]

Serve the Lord with gladness! Come into his presence with singing!

Saranam, Saranam, Saranam

Know that the Lord is God! It is He who made us, and we are His; we are His people, and the sheep of His pasture.

Saranam, Saranam, Saranam

Enter His gates with thanksgiving, and His courts with praise! Give thanks to Him, bless His name!

Saranam, Saranam, Saranam

For the Lord is good; His steadfast love endures forever, and His faithfulness to all generations.

Saranam, Saranam, Saranam

Come let us worship God together, let us celebrate God's presence with us, and let us rejoice with each other.

Saranam, Saranam, Saranam

Sisters and brothers, today we all are historically united in witnessing the love of God publicly. Let us thank God, look upon Him and listen to His voice. May we, those who are gathered here, receive the guidance of His Spirit. Let us be empowered to speak to the whole Church and make known the divine will.

---

[2] "Saranam" = refuge

May we all be strengthened in our spiritual life and perfected in our witness and service.

PRAYER OF THANKSGIVING

O God our Creator, we praise You and thank You for creating us in Your image. We praise You for calling us to be partners in constructing the reign of God with the values of love, peace and justice here on earth. We thank You for Your promise of being with us always as we counter and confront the gods of this world in their manifestations of corruption, fundamentalism, communalism, patriarchal structures, casteism, stigma and discrimination.

We thank You for Your son Jesus who always challenges us to live in solidarity with the least, homeless and the needy, the lost and the betrayed and the last and those at the edges of Church and society.

We thank You for Your empowering and counselling Spirit who help us to embrace new dreams, new visions, new ideas, and new plans to reflect and articulate Your prophetic voice on the earth.

We thank You for Your commission to plant and pluck, to construct and break down, to create and destroy and to overthrow powers and structures that create divisions based on ecclesial confessions, denominations and theologies.

We thank You for making us be part of this gathering. Lead us to be committed to Your reign, to bring justice where there is injustice, peace where there is violence, freedom where there is bondage, and love where there is ill will.

Alleluia (7 times)

SCRIPTURE READING (The Word of God in Context)

Every scripture reading will follow a real life experience.

Wealth and Just-living (Real-life Experience): Experience of people displaced and forced to migrate, as well as threatened of their safety and peace, due to the construction of nuclear power plants, shall be shared here.

Related Canonised Scripture   I Kings 10: 1-25

The Earth is the Lord's (Real-life Experience): Experience of Indigenous People, displaced and forced to migrate, as well as threatened of their access to their land, due to the construction of factories by the by multinational companies, shall be shared here.

Related Canonised Scripture   Romans 8: 17-24

Glory to God and Peace on Earth (Real-life Experience): Experience of local people, displaced and forced to migrate, as well as threatened of their freedom and fundamental rights, due to unjust government policies, acts and laws, shall be shared here.

Related Canonised Scripture   Luke 4: 16-20

Before the sermon, a special song related to the theme shall be sung or a folk song or a dance from any communities living under subjugation can be presented here.

HOMILY   The Gospel in a Groaning World

AFFIRMATION OF FAITH *(In unison)*

We believe in God the Creator,

who created and is creating everything:

the universe, the world, the plants wond animals, and us;

each of us, unique, individual and beloved of God.

We believe in God the Christ,
who liberates and intercedes and groans for everything:
the universe, the world, the plants and animals, and us:
each of us, unique, individual and beloved of the Christ.

We believe in God the Holy Spirit,
who guides and groans along with everything:
the universe, the world, the plants and animals, and us;
each of us, unique, individual and beloved of the Spirit.

We believe in one Church a body of God
Who is present among us,
working directly in our lives, society and the entire creation
towards liberation.

As the Church, we groan and work for justice and peace,
forgiving, healing, touching everyone,
never rejecting any who willingly receive
this freely offered gift of love and grace and fullness of life. **Amen**

CONFESSION OF SIN

Most merciful, forgiving God, we confess to You, to one another and to other creatures, that we have sinned by what we have done and by what we have left undone. We have not loved You, our neighbours and other creatures with our whole heart and mind and strength. We have not always had in us the mind of Christ. You alone know how often we have made You groan by sinning against You and Your creation, by wandering from Your ways. Forgive us.

We pray to You, gracious God. Free us from our sins of stigma, discrimination, untouchability, endorsing the powerful, not identifying and accompanying the human and nature communities who groan for freedom. Renew us with Your forgiving grace and the strength of Your Holy Spirit, for the sake of Jesus Christ your Son our Saviour. Amen.

ABSOLUTION

God has accepted your prayers of confessions and absolves you of all your offences!

Remember, God groans with you when you groan for your sins.

Remember, God works out liberation and healing when you groan and give yourselves to God's purposes.

This identifying, forgiving, reforming, renewing God will continue to accompany you. **Amen**

INTERCESSORY PRAYERS

O God, we pray for the Global Church and the Ecumenical Movement that they may be just and inclusive and have a sense of responsibility in sharing Your liberative values and motives among the earth communities as mutually groaning and accompanying partners.

Khumbhaya Lord, Khumbhaya *(Singing)*

God of peace and justice, we pray for our country India. We groan for peace, especially in Kashmir, Northeast India, Chhattisgarh and other places where people are made to live under subjugating laws and threatening weapons.

Khumbhaya Lord, Khumbhaya *(Singing)*

God of life and justice, we pray that You touch and transform all those forces which make the Church and society to be subject to unjust practices of exclusion such as casteism, untouchability and communalism. We pray for the experience of "just-equality" of all human and other earth communities, who are deprived of the right to life, learning and livelihood. Primarily, we remember the struggling communities in Jagatsinghpur district in Odisha, Kudankulam in Tamil Nadu, and other parts of the country where they are subject to diabolic laws and dominant socio-economic and political structures.

Khumbhaya Lord, Khumbhaya *(Singing)*

God of communities, we pray for all ecumenical organisations in India and their constituent members. We pray for local congregations and their Sextons, Deacons, Elders, Catechists, Bible Women, Missionaries, Clergies and Bishops and all service and leadership givers. May our Christian calling and commitment to the mission of God be expressed in ways that bear witness to the gospel of Christ and not to our narrow ecclesial organisational structuralism. God of grace, enable us to break all barriers and limitations and to make Churches without walls, which embrace people who live on the edges and outside the margins of society.

Khumbhaya Lord, Khumbhaya *(Singing)*

HYMN *(In unison)*
(While the hymn is sung, a piece of bread would be distributed to all the delegates. Kindly hold the bread, knowing and believing in faith that we are partaking in God's fellowship meal.)

Ever and always be praise,
Eternal Lord to Thee–ever

and always be praise.
Boundless with mercy
Thy arms are encircling us, (repeat)
Ceaseless with praise with
our songs we'll encompass Thee.
Ever and always be praise.

Healing He brings in His train,
He knows our weaknesses–healing
He brings in His train.
Sins are forgiven and
our souls are revived again, (repeat)
Sonship restored and
their salvation brought to men.
Ever and always be praise.

As east is far from the west,
So far our transgressions–
as east is far from the west,
Have been removed, and
His mercy made manifest, (repeat)
Judgment delivered for all
them that are oppressed.
Ever and always be praise.

Life like the grass will decay,
Like flowers will pass away–life
like the grass will decay,
But will not wither where held by

His faithfulness, (repeat)
Faith clingeth fast to
His unwearied changelessness.
Ever and always be praise.

Throned in the heavens, He is Lord,
Through ages changelessly–throned
in the heavens He is Lord.
Blessed through all
generations eternally, (repeat)
Bless Him my soul,
in thy Saviour rejoicing thee
Ever and always be praise.

The Resurrected Christ is here
His Spirit is with us.

Lift up your hearts
We lift them to the Lord.

Post Resurrection Food-Fellowship
Experience of Christ and Disciples

Luke 24: 25-36 (NRSV)

(V. 25) Then He (Jesus) said to them. "Oh, how foolish you are, and how slow of heart to believe all that prophets have declared! (V. 26) Was it not Messiah should suffer these things and enter to the glory"? (V. 27) Then beginning with Moses and all the prophets, He interpreted to them the things about himself in all the scriptures. (V. 28) As they came near the village to which they were going, He walked ahead as if He was going on. (V. 29) But they urged him strongly, saying, "Stay with us, because it is almost evening and the day is nearly over." So he went in to stay with them. (V.30) When He was at the table with them, He took bread and blessed and broke it, and gave it to them. (V.31) Then their eyes were opened, and they recognized him; and He vanished from their sights. (v. 32) They said to each other "Were not our hearts burning within us on the road, while He was talking to us on the road, while He was opening the Scriptures to us?" (V.33) That same hour they got up and returned to Jerusalem: and they found the eleven and their companions gathered together. (V. 34) They were saying, "The Lord appeared to Simon!" (V.35) Then they told what had happened on the road, and how He had been made known to them in the breaking of the bread.

Silence

In this fellowship, we accept that which God gives us, become that which God makes of us and render it up. Indeed in this fellowship, the whole of what our faith means is expressed. That which otherwise we would apprehend piecemeal is integrated into our faith expressions which present it all as the sheer gift of God. On any one occasion, we may be conscious only of this or that element in the meaning, but it is all there because God in Christ is there. In dependence on God for everything, we render it all back to God in thankful adoration. (C. H. Dodd)

Let us pray in unison. While the following prayer is prayed, let us lift the bread.

Our God, our life, we as Your communities who have faith in the resurrected Christ come together and bless these loaves of bread which are brought for the fellowship meal. God of all, we break this bread in Your Son's name to strengthen our

fellowship. **We have come as helpless and hopeful people. In Your name we share, eat and live to bear witness to You. In the name of the resurrected Christ, we pray, O God, our parent. Amen.**

The bread which is in our hand shall be consumed as a symbolic action that we are part of resurrected Jesus' fellowship.

AFTER THE FELLOWSHIP MEAL

Having now in faith joined in the fellowship meal, let us pray together,

Almighty God, we thank You for uniting us through this fellowship meal in the name of Your Son Jesus Christ. Amen.

Through Him we offer You ourselves to be a living witness. Send us out to the community to establish Your fellowship by the power of Your Spirit to live and work to Your praise and glory. Amen.

BENEDICTION

When the song of the choir is over,
When the preaching is over,
When the congregation disappears,
When the altar elements are kept in place,
When the ministers return home,

The work of the Christian begins:
To find the lost, to heal the broken, to accompany the needy,
To uphold the human rights,
To release the bonded, to rebuild societies,

To bring peace among communities,
To care for the whole earth.

May the peace of God which passes all understanding keep your hearts and minds in the knowledge and love of God and of his Son, Jesus Christ our Lord. The blessings of God Almighty, the Father, the Son, and the Holy Spirit be among you and remain with you always. **Amen.**

7

Celebrating Faith by Witnessing:
A Liturgy for the Dalit Liberation Day[1]

INTRODUCTION

The Faith of Dalit Christians: A Threshold of Liberation

Caste discrimination marks the lives of Dalits even within the fold of the Church. As one of the bishops in the Church of South India (CSI) from Vellore rightly pointed out at the World Council of Churches (WCC), "We feel we have more in common with Dalits of other faiths than with Christians of 'upper caste groups!; the Dalits feel alienated within the Church because of casteism. But at the same time, they realise that the faith they cling to within the fold of Christianity is all about liberation

---

[1] *For the National Coordination Committee for Dalit Christian Rights (NCCDC), a joint programme of the National Council of Churches in India and the Catholic Bishops' Conference of India (CBCI), this liturgy was prepared by J.W. Vinod, K. Immanuel Paul Vivekanandh, A. Jeevaraj, Henry Jacob J., and Asha B. The team was headed by Sunil Raj Philip. The liturgy published here is its modified version.*

and of a 'new heaven and new earth.'" So, the lives of Dalit Christians become more of a struggle towards liberation. They find rays of hope in the preferential option of Jesus Christ. Dalit Christians celebrate their faith by witnessing through their own life, which is of struggles, daring the discrimination they face, the pathetic conditions of the lives most of them live, and the exclusion they suffer in different fields.

Dalit Christians: Facing Double Discrimination

Being the most complicated and hierarchical social system of the world, casteism makes Dalits vulnerable. It creates barriers for them to have upward mobility in the social ladder. Dalit Christians also share the same struggle of their brothers and sisters from other faiths. But, they are deprived of the constitutional right of the reservation system only because they have moved to the fold of Christianity. It is important to note that the National Council of Churches in India (NCCI), along with the Catholic Bishops' Conference of India (CBCI), has been leading the struggle and advocacy for the repealing of the infamous Presidential Order that was instrumental in denying the Scheduled Caste status for Dalits who were converted to Christianity and Islam.

It is very important for Dalit Christians in terms of the struggle for reservation. They express their faith in God the liberator through this struggle for constitutional rights. Indian Churches have the responsibility to take part in this struggle in solidarity with Dalit Christians to achieve their goal.

Dalit Liberation Sunday: Expression of Faith

Dalit Liberation Sunday, an initiative of the NCCI, was later taken up on a larger scale by the National Coordination Committee for Dalit Christian Rights (NCCDC), a joint programme of the NCCI and the CBCI, aimed at the empowerment of local congregations for Dalit liberation. Dalit Liberation Sunday is celebrated across India by the member Churches of the NCCI and the Churches under the CBCI on the Sunday nearest to the International Human Rights Day (IHRD, 10 December) commemorating its significance in Indian Dalit struggles.

Let us celebrate our faith

Let us join together to celebrate our faith in the liberator God. As part of the celebration let us,

1. Take a bold stand against various forms of casteism within the Church.

2. Support and take part in the struggle of Dalit Christians for the constitutional rights of reservation.

3. Design study programmes in groups such as Sunday School, Youth Fellowship, etc., with a biblical base of exhortation against casteism.

4. Use Christian institutions to provide ample education for Dalits who face discrimination even in the field of education.

5. Vehemently condemn various atrocities committed against Dalits across India.

We are happy to present this booklet to the Indian Churches, which contains ideas for Dalit Liberation Sunday worship, to be used in the local congregations. Local Churches can take the freedom to adapt/ enhance/ or use parts of the worship order without losing the essence of the worship order. We request you to send us the feedback after the observance of this particular Sunday.

Let us celebrate our faith by witnessing together!

ENACTMENT

A group of people can beat "parai" (drums chiefly played by Dalits) with dance and enter the Church. They dance their way to the front of the altar or the chairperson's table showing their respect and inviting God to their presence. Then a Dalit family can walk forward with gift/s such as rice gruel in a pot, vegetables, cereals, etc., as an offering to God. Then some "upper" caste people may "disturb" the gathering and shout, "You low caste people, stop your offering; you are polluted." This would definitely cause a commotion. The Dalits shout back and say, "Are we not created in the image of God? How long can you deny our rights? Is not showing love witnessing to God? Where is your witness? Answer us…answer us…." The "upper" caste people remain silent. Then the Dalit family shall say "play the parai… Nobody can deny our rights… Let us worship God."

INVOCATION

(Beat the sound of "Parai" for invoking the presence of God)

We beat the sound of pain
Come O God, give us healing. (Beat *Parai*)

We beat the sound of justice.
Come O God, lead us to freedom. (Beat *Parai*)

We beat the sound of reconciliation.
Come O God, restore peace. (Beat *Parai*)

We beat the sound of faith.
Come O God, make us holy. (Beat *Parai*)

We beat the sound of unity.
Come O God, strengthen us. (Beat *Parai*)

OPENING PRAYER *(In unison)*
Loving God, our helper, redeemer and our co-traveller, our beginning and our end, we thank You for accepting our gathering and being present in our midst. Let Your holy presence renew us and enable us to envision a life of freedom and equality, breaking the barriers of caste which divides and discriminates us. Through this worship and in our lives give us Your strength not to serve caste but Your Son and our Saviour Jesus Christ. We genuinely believe that by Your empowering presence, we will worship You and work towards a world filled with justice and peace. *Amen*.

OPENING SONG *(Set to the tune of "Standing on the Promises of Christ my Lord")*

Standing as the witnesses of our Christ the friend
In our pain and pathos we will share His strength;
By attaining freedom we will shout and sing,
Standing as the witnesses of God.

Chorus
Standing, standing
Standing as the witnesses of Christ our Saviour;
Standing, standing,
We're standing as the witnesses of God.

Standing firmly in struggles that cannot fail,
Even when the storms of doubt and fear assail,

By the living Word of God we shall prevail,
Standing as the witnesses of God.
Chorus

Standing as the witnesses of Christ the Lord,
Bound in love and trust each other as strong cord,
In communion we shall find a joyful life,
Standing as the witnesses of God.
Chorus

Standing to the calling which we cannot fail,
Listening every moment to the people's wail,
Working ceaseless for the justice all day long,
Standing as the witnesses of God.
Chorus

CONFESSION

*(A cardboard box can be kept in front of the altar.
A piece of paper can be distributed to everyone.
After confession, people can write "we condemn caste practice,"
and as an act of discarding caste, the papers can be crushed
and thrown into the box.)*

Member 1:   Broken hearts, rejected skin, silenced voices, molested bodies, and devalued wisdom have been the realities of Dalit communities for ages. Our false beliefs rooted in discriminatory caste systems have prejudiced our minds to divide ourselves based on discriminative works and colours. We are yet to completely recognise the "imago dei" in all of us and especially in our Dalit brothers and sisters. Rejecting our neighbours is rejecting God.

Forgive us, O Lord, for we have failed to recognise Your image in others. Renew our minds to accept each other. We sincerely repent for being casteist in our lives.

Member 2:   Expressing sympathy, being neutrally silent, engaging in divided arguments and practising compassionless negligence have often been our response to the brutal murder, rapes, beatings and violence on Dalit communities. Unlike our saviour Jesus who stood with "Dalits" of His time, we have failed to strongly identify with the struggles of the suffering humanity, to maintain the status quo. Silence has often been our answer for the violence on our Dalit friends.

Forgive us, O Lord, for we have been silent to the cries of pain and suffering. Disturb us in our silence, strengthen and unify us to stand up for justice. We sincerely repent for our negligent attitude.

Member 3:   Worship, praise, prayers and greetings have been the only mark of our Churches today. While recognising the good works of many in trying to make a casteless Church we are still a casteist Church. While we believe in widening our boundaries, we are still shrinking in our witness to be a casteless community. Selective and suspicious inclusion and charity-based expression have often been our approach in accepting our Dalit friends into the Church community.

Forgive us, O Lord, for we are still a caste-based faith community. Continually pour out your spirit of unity and oneness. We sincerely repent for failing to witness as a casteless community.

SCRIPTURE READING

Deuteronomy 1: 13-18

Acts of the Apostles 4: 13-22

Luke 11: 45-54

REFLECTION   Celebrating Faith by Witnessing

FAITH AFFIRMATION

We believe in God who created us "as equals" in His image. We believe in God, who is disturbed by our cries, takes side with the oppressed and struggles with us in our resilience against caste discrimination.

We believe and follow Jesus, the Christ and the incarnated one, our Immanuel, who teaches us to love, who gives us the courage to take up our cross and follow him to stand against the caste structures that oppress. We believe in Him who was crucified for rebelling against oppression; we believe that by His death and resurrection, we find hope in ourselves that we will be resurrected from all bondage as free people.

We believe in the enlightening and empowering power of the Holy Spirit, who nurtures us to stand against injustice. We believe that her uniting strength will fill our minds and bodies for united efforts in working towards justice for Dalit communities in all aspects of life.

We believe in the courageous and prophetic efforts of subaltern saints who, through their life and witness, stand firm against the caste practices in the Church and society and continuously live out their prophetic calling to create a just society.

We believe in the "called out" peoples' movement, the Church, which continues to witness the Dalit Christ in its firm

stand against caste discrimination, denial, subjugation and marginalisation. We believe that this "called out" community continues to embrace and accommodate and live for broken bodies in our midst.

We believe in the everlasting life without any discrimination and oppression, but a renewed life with freedom and mutual sharing. Amen.

OFFERTORY AND COMMITMENT SONG[2]

Deep in the human heart
The fire of justice burns;
A vision of a world renewed
Through radical concern
As Christians we are called
To set the captives free,
To overthrow the evil powers
And end hypocrisy;

This is our task today to
Build a world of peace;
A world of justice, freedom, truth
Where kindness will increase;
A world from hunger freed,
A world where people share,
Where every person is of
Worth and no one live in fear.

---

[2] By William Livingstone Wallace

Taking the step of faith,
We leave the past behind
And move into the future
World with open heart and mind
By grace we work with Christ,
As one community,
To bring new hope
And fuller life to all humanity.

INTERCESSORY PRAYERS *(Pray in silence after each voice, remembering people/communities represented by the voices)*

Voice 1: I am a Dalit Christian who struggled my entire life with two identities: as a member of the Scheduled Caste community and as a Christian. I have struggled to avail myself of fee concession and scholarship. We did not have any other option because I belong to a poor agricultural labourer family, and my parents were not able to spend money on exorbitant fees. Therefore, they asked us to say without guilt that "I'm a Scheduled Caste in my school." But, I was reluctant, and I couldn't celebrate my faith when I was undergoing these kinds of struggles. That incident compelled me to ask why I was born a Dalit Christian in this caste-based society. I still have the guilty feeling that I am not able to celebrate my faith in life and economically uplift my family.

Silence

Voice 2: I am a Dalit woman. I face discrimination every day for being a Dalit and a woman. I cannot bear to see my children being discriminated by my upper caste neighbours in not being allowed to play with their children. I have always felt that the upper caste people have forgotten the fact that all of us live on the same earth and share water and foodgrains for our survival. We live under the threat of being molested in caste violence, and many a time our men in our own families dominate us. Many a time we cry in solitude with no support, but only loneliness surrounds us.

Silence

Voice 3: I am an uneducated man and working as a manual scavenger for the past 15 years. I was supporting my family with the little money I got whenever I had work. One day, my friend and I refused to get into the septic tank, but our owner forced us to enter inside and clean it properly. While we were cleaning the septic tank, unfortunately, my friend died when some poisonous substance was released from the tank. Now his family is abandoned. I plead with you to consider your fellow Dalit humans with dignity. There are still Dalit workers engaged in manual cleaning of pits and public toilets, and their socio-economic mobility is still a distant dream for members of the lower castes. Who will hear our cry? Where is justice?

Silence

Voice 4: My friend and I were thrilled and enthusiastic young people who were born in Dalit families. One day a girl belonging to an "upper caste" community liked my friend and proposed to him. Both of them loved each other very deeply, and caste was never a barrier for them. But trouble came when their parents and the community members came to know about it. They threatened to kill my friend. Hence, both of them decided to get married without the consent of the girl's family. Enraged with anger, the "upper caste" community burnt our villages, and to the shock of all of us, the father of the girl died by suicide.

We decided to protect the couple. We were willing to sacrifice our own lives. However, soon my friend was arrested on false charges. The girl was separated from him, and ultimately my friend was found dead on a railway track. We all suspect that this was murder. But our voices are silenced.

Silence

THE LORD'S PRAYER (in vernacular)

CLOSING PRAYER *(In unison)*

O Lord, the One who was born as a poor "Dalit" in a colonised land; lived with the marginalised and the oppressed; for the sake of justice, died between criminals and died amidst the cries of many "Dalits"; resurrected to live victoriously and eternally; Christ our friend, comrade and saviour, we commit all of us into Your hands. As we leave from here, we pray that we will recognise in the bodies of others Your presence, especially those who are abused and slandered. Help us to live Your word, and express love and justice to everyone around us. We pray for Your continued presence in encouraging us to bear witness to justice and truth along with all the people who struggle for peace, especially for the Dalit and subaltern communities all over the world. Amen.

BENEDICTION

Go out into the world as witness of truth and justice. Let the Triune God nurture us, strengthen us and unite us to be a "disturbing presence" to injustice and a "comforting presence" to all who seek love and peace. **Amen.**

———————

8

Justice for Dalits: A Call for Solidarity[1]

(Dalit folk music will be played, during which the participants will be seated in a circle and shall prepare themselves for worship. An urn of black powder is placed at the entrance of the worship hall, and members are requested to make a cross or any other mark on themselves. The mark of black powder on each of us is a symbolic expression for our solidarity with our Dalit brothers and sisters and symbolic expression to reveal our willingness to perceive and address the Dalit cause towards transformation.)

CALL TO WORSHIP

Jesus said, "For where two or three are gathered together in my name, there am I in the midst of them" (Saint Matthew 18:20).

God who is revealed in a human man Jesus Christ,

---

[1] *This liturgy (including the songs), prepared by Raj Bharat Patta, was used at the "Global Ecumenical Conference on Justice for Dalits–A Call for Solidarity" held at Bangkok, Thailand, 21–24 March 2009. The liturgy published here is a modified version.*

Where are You, O God, when our people are inhumanly discriminated in the name of caste?

Where are You, O God, when our people are crying for life due to increasing violence and cruelty?

Where are You, O God, when our people are trampled under the rubric of casteism, fundamentalism, patriarchy and communalism?

Where are You O God, when our people are denied access to water in the name of caste, privatisation and consumerism?

Come now, O God,
Come into our midst to inspire us to be Your advocates for justice
Come now, O God,
Come into our midst to challenge us to be Your channels of equality
Come now, O God,
Come into our midst to transform us to be Your beacons of transformation.
Come now, O God,
Come into our midst to quench our thirst by filling us with Your life-giving waters
Come now, O God,
Come into our midst and grant access to safe drinking waters to our Dalit and Adivasi people
Come now, O God,
Come into our midst to make us realise that as a human family, whether we live upstream or downstream, we are all in the same boat.

CONGREGATIONAL HYMN

When I needed a neighbour, were you there, were you there
When I needed a neighbour were you there?

Chorus   *And the caste and the colour*
                  and the name won't matter,
                  Were you there?

I was hungry and thirsty, were you there, were you there?
I was hungry and thirsty, were you there?

I was cold, I was naked, were you there, were you there?
I was cold, I was naked, were you there?

When I needed a shelter, were you there, were you there?
When I needed a shelter, were you there?

When I needed a healer, were you there, were you there?
When I needed a healer, were you there?

Wherever you travel I'll be there, I'll be there
Wherever you travel I'll be there.

ENACTMENT OF THE SCRIPTURE

Mark 7: 31-37 Advocacy of "Ephphatha Community"
for Healing

TESTIMONIES OF FAITH & AFFIRMATIONS OF FAITH[2]

I

When they (Hindu fanatics) came for Narmada Digal, she
wasn't there. She had fled, five children and mother-in-law in

---

[2] Names changed

tow, to the safety of the jungle a kilometre away. So, they set ablaze what she left behind, a framed picture of Jesus, a Bible in Oriya, utensils in the kitchen, some clothes, and linen. By the time Narmada tiptoed back, her home was gone. What was left was still hot from the ashes, and smoking. The neighbours came to commiserate. Narmada took a good look, stood erect, and pulled her sari over her head. She began to pray, "Lord, forgive us our sins. Jesus, You are the only one. Save us from our misfortune. Free us, Lord." The words came tumbling out. Narmada's children joined her. She was weeping as she pleaded for deliverance. So was everybody else. It's a simple bond that no human wrath can sever the relationship between a woman and her God. "I will die. But I won't stop being a Christian," Narmada says. A staunch and brave Dalit Christian woman! She is not a "rice Christian" but on the contrary, a Christian very rich in faith. The flames of communal passion cannot consume the deep faith of Dalit and Tribal Christians.

As we listen to this testimony of faith, we affirm that
We believe in God, in whom all faiths originate, exist, nurture and sustain,
We believe in God, who transforms chaos into order
We believe in God, who creates all beings in equality
We commend the faith of our sister Narmada,
We commit ourselves to fight against the forces of fundamentalism, casteism, communalism and patriarchy on our Dalit friends,
We commit to stand by our Dalit brothers and sisters in their times of toil and tribulations.

II

Manohar, a Christian of Dalit origin, has been regular at the Church services. He is the only one who became Christian, and the rest of his family members are still under the aegis of their previous faith. For Manohar, Christianity was liberative from the evil clutches of caste. His son Timothy was raised as a Dalit Christian and on one occasion was beaten up severely by his classmates in a clash over college elections. They humiliated him in the name of caste. When Manohar and Timothy approached the police station to file a case against them, the police refused to file a lawsuit against on those "high" caste people. Besides this, the police told them that on becoming Christians, they were no longer Dalits and such atrocities on them could not be covered under the prescribed "Scheduled Castes and Scheduled Tribes Prevention of Atrocities Act." Timothy asked his father, "Why are we discriminated in the name of caste? Don't we have the freedom to practice the faith of our choice? From where does justice come to us in situations of violence?" Manohar answered, "Our help comes from God in whom we have our faith." The bleeding Timothy today is the crucified Christ then, and we shall fight back for justice and our rights. The denial of constitutional justice cannot consume the deep faith of our Dalit Christians.

As we listen to this testimony of faith, we affirm that

We believe in Jesus Christ, the one who is crucified every day as our Dalit brothers and sisters are beaten and bruised,

We believe in the resurrection of Jesus Christ where the clutches of oppression and death are chained in His empty tomb,

We believe in the coming of Jesus Christ who shall come to give sight to the blind and blind those who see.

We believe in the Holy Spirit, the advocate for justice, and the one who accompanies all those struggling in their journey for liberation,

We believe in the Holy Spirit, who convinces all the faithful to advocate for the rights of Dalits and who inspires us to be in solidarity with them,

We believe in community living, where all creation will live in peace and harmony without any stratification, domination and hegemony.

We commend the faith of our brothers Manohar and Timothy,

We commit ourselves to advocate for the equal rights of Christians and Muslims of Dalit origin, and pledge to be with them in overcoming violence of all forms,

We commit ourselves to participate in the struggles of our Dalit people and strive for life to be celebrated in all fullness here and now.

(Here, each participant shall tie a knot of the one end of the ribbon given with the ribbon of their neighbour sitting next to them to form a "Circle of Solidarity and Advocacy.")

PRAYERS FOR THE CIRCLE OF SOLIDARITY AND ADVOCACY

Encircle us O God, as we form a circle of solidarity and advocacy for the cause of Dalits.

Engage us O God, as we pledge to lobby and advocate for the rights of Dalits.

Enlighten us O God, as we perceive the Dalit cause as a faith issue and justice issue.

Enable us O God, as we proclaim to be bold in condemning all forces of caste as sin.

Empower us O God, as we build communities of equality, peace and reconciliation.

Entrust us O God, as we assemble to be the firm channels of hope and liberation.

Enthuse us O God, as we join hands in continuing the reign of God here on earth.

Enliven us O God, as we commit to strive for the celebration of life for all in fullness.

Enlarge and deepen our fellowship and friendship so that we all remain faithful and truthful to the calling and commitment of Dalit solidarity and transformation.

Entice us with Your grace in all our endeavours for transformation and liberation. In Christ's name, we ask these our prayers. Amen.

CLOSING PRAYER (*Rereading of the Lord's Prayer from a Dalit perspective*)

Our God who is present everywhere, particularly in the struggles of our people,

Let our acts of justice and truth proclaim Your name,

Help us to realise Your sovereignty by being in solidarity with one another,

Inspire us to do Your will, the will for transformation and Your willingness to die for us, on this earth, as You practised,

Gives us daily Your knowledge to share our food, resources and ourselves with others, as You share them with us,

Lead us not into the temptation of practising caste and being self-centred,

Deliver us from all kinds of oppression and discrimination,

For, Your reign, power & glory shall come unto us when all of us live in the spirit of a community governed by mutual dignity, respect and equality. Amen.

BENEDICTION

May God, who created us all in God's equal image,

May Jesus Christ, who was in total solidarity with the struggling creation,

May the Holy Spirit, who advocates justice to all creation

Continue to inspire, challenge and transform each of us here to go into the world to preach, profess and practise the values of God's reign and to strive for a just and inclusive community in our localities. **Amen**

(As sign of receiving a new hope to be the hope in transforming our community, sprouted seeds are shared and distributed to all members.)

COMMUNITY SONG OF SOLIDARITY[3]

Jesus Christ is waiting
Waiting in the streets
No one is his neighbour

---

[3] Text by John L. Bell & Graham Maule; Tune: Noel Nouvelet (11.10.11.10)

All alone he eats
Listen, Lord Jesus
I am lonely too
Make me friend or stranger
Fit to wait on you

Jesus Christ is healing
Healing in the streets
Curing those who suffer
Touching those he greets
Listen, Lord Jesus
I have pity too
Let me care be active
Healing just like you

Jesus Christ is raging
Raging in the streets
Where injustice spirals
And real hope retreats
Listen, Lord Jesus
I am angry too
In the Kingdom's causes
Let me rage with you.

———————

9

Solidarity in Christ:
Bearing One Another's Burdens[1]

DIRECTIONS FOR WORSHIP LEADERS

- *Please feel free to adapt this worship order as the Spirit leads you and in ways that are appropriate to your context. Since many Tribal Churches do not follow a formal liturgy, worship leaders are advised to adapt creatively the content and the principles of the proposed worship order in your respective local settings.*

- *Leaders who will be initiating the worship are requested to prayerfully go through the document before using it in your respective congregations.*

- *Worship place could be decorated with artifacts, plants*

---

[1] *This liturgy, based on Galatians 6:2, was prepared by Pangenungba Kechu and Renemsongla Ozukum, members of the Nagaland Baptist Church Council, and was used in all the constituent bodies of the National Council of Churches in India during the 'Tribal and Adivasi Sunday.' The liturgy published here is its modified version.*

and flowers that are connected to Adivasi, Tribal and Indigenous peoples.

- *Musical instruments such as the tambourine, flute and drum may be arranged and played during the worship service.*

- *Tribal and Adivasi ways of chanting, singing, dancing and drumming can be done using an LCD projector or enacted by different groups.*

THE ACT OF CONGREGATING FOR WORSHIP

The world belongs to God, and all the people of many races, tribes, tongues and cultures.

How good and lovely it is to worship God together. We are all the children of God.

Fathers and mothers, sisters and brothers, boys and girls, clergy and laity, we have come here to worship God who offers us freedom through our Lord Christ Jesus.

For the Spirit of life in God has set us free from the law and the sin of death.

In the name of the living God, I call all people of God to prayerfully join in celebrating the struggles and hopes of our Adivasi and Tribal communities.

We prepare our hearts and minds so that we can connect with the stories of our fellow sisters and brothers.

As followers of the Way, we bring our strengths and limitations under the redeeming cross of Jesus Christ.

As partakers of Your body, O Christ, may Your spirit unite

us to share the burdens and dreams of Adivasi Churches and communities.

If convenient, let us all stand for the opening song.

OPENING SONG (*Set to the tune of the Hymn "Love Divine all Love Excelling"*)[2]

Help us build a Christian Fam'ly
God most loving and gracious.
With love break existing barriers
To bear a Christian witness.
Help us build a new society
Where the pride of sex and race,
Colour, caste, class disparity
Will be wiped out with much ease.

Help us build a Christian fam'ly
God most loving and gracious.
Help us work with hope, peace, and trust
Confidence and love precious.
Stand together against evil
Hand in hand for good and just,
Make our visions and dreams come true
That each fam'ly abide in you.

Help us build a Christian fam'ly
With new values and with love.
With our partners, parents, children

---

[2] Text by Charles Wesley (1747); Tune: *Beecher* (8.7.8.7 D), composed by John Zundel

Nature and with you above.
Celebrate the newness of life
Bring forth peace and harmony
Through your Holy presence with us
And your overwhelming grace

Kindly be seated

PRAYER OF THANKSGIVING AND ASPIRATION

Clergy/Male: We thank You, O God, for inspiring our visionary leaders to form the National Council of Churches in India (NCCI) in 1914.

All: **May the grace and prophetic spirit of God continue to empower the leaders of the NCCI.**

Female: In particular, we pray that You will continue to bless the activities of the Tribal and Adivasi ministry in NCCI.

All: **May Your spirit guide the leaders of the Tribal and Adivasi ministry in the NCCI.**

Male: Our hearts are filled with gratitude for the missionaries and evangelists who have toiled hard to establish Adivasi and Tribal Churches for Your glory.

All: **May You help all of us to appreciate our Christian heritage and take pride in our Christian identity.**

SCRIPTURE READINGS

Old Testament   Micah 6:8

Epistle   Galatians 6:2

Gospel   Saint Mark 9: 33-35

REFLECTION Solidarity in Christ: Bearing One Another's Burdens

CONFESSION

Come, let us confess the indifference that has kept us away from the struggles of Adivasis and Indigenous peoples.

Loving God, open our eyes from the inhuman act of sleepiness and allow Your spirit to shake up our frozen Christian consciences.

O God, teach us to translate our spirit of solidarity into genuine acts of accountability.

Help us to pray following the model of Jesus: praying to God in solidarity with people around us.

We invoke Your Spirit to enable us to pray in conversation with the lived realities of the Adivasi people.

Teach us how to pray in ways that would allow us to affirm and heal the burdens of our fellow members in Christ.

In saying the Lord's Prayer, I cannot say, *'Our'*

If my faith has no space for the Adivasi, Tribal and Indigenous communities.

I cannot say, *'Father'*

If I do not treat them as my Christian brothers and sisters.

I cannot say, *'who art in heaven'*

If I cannot share the plight of thousands of Adivasi who do not have land and space to live on earth.

I cannot say, *'hallowed be Thy name'*
If I, who am called by God's name, am not holy.

I cannot say, *'Thy will be done'*
If I am so focused on my own selfish will. God of justice, what kind of prayer should I say when the will and aspirations of Tribal people are crushed mercilessly every day?

I cannot say, *'on earth as it is in heaven'*
Unless I am genuinely ready to bear the burden of my Adivasi Christian friends.

I cannot say, *'Give us this day our daily bread'*
If I continue to accumulate and fail to share my resources with the Tribal families who are going hungry every day.

I cannot say, *'Forgive us our debts as we forgive our debtors'*
If I continue to harbour hatred against the rebellions and revolts of Tribal communities.

I cannot say, *'Lead us not into temptation'*
If I continue to remain in a situation where I am likely to be tempted to participate in denying the rights of Indigenous peoples.

I cannot say, *'Deliver us from evil'*
If I am not prepared to stand for the social, economic and political emancipation of the Adivasis and Tribal Christians.

I cannot say, *'Thine is the kin(g)dom'*
If I fear what my friends, Church and community would say when I speak about the rights and inclusion of alienated Indigenous Christians.

I cannot say, *'Thine is the glory'*
If I keep glorifying my Church and seek my own glory.

I cannot say, *'forever'*
If I cannot trust in You and become too anxious and preoccupied with temporal affairs.

I cannot say, *'**Amen**'*
Unless I can honestly say, 'Cost what it may, this is my prayer.'

ASSURANCE OF FORGIVENESS

Living God, we thank You for speaking to us through Your Spirit to discern our sins. We are assured that, if we seek You in truth, we receive forgiveness of our sins through the life and death of Your son Jesus Christ. (John 3:16)

Truly, we do not want our apology to be mere words but a genuine lament for our inaction and insensitivity.

We ask forgiveness for all our shortcomings, even as we pledge to forgive our fellow Christian friends. (Matthew 18: 21-22)

Help us to forgive because we are a forgiven community in Christ. Help us to reconcile and bear each other's burdens as we have been reconciled through Your Son Jesus Christ. (II Corinthians 5:17-20)

AFFIRMATION OF FAITH *(All stand, if convenient)*

We believe in the God who created dynamic and inclusive human communities, the beautiful planet earth, and all living creatures. We acknowledge that it is God who gives life to the forests, rivers and land that sustain the Indigenous communities. We affirm that God is the source of life amidst abundant food and waste, as well as poverty and hunger. In a context of religious vigilantism, we renew our courage to worship God without any fear and intimidation.

We believe in Jesus Christ, the only Son of God, born of the virgin Mary. We discern that the Church is called to serve as a witness to the life, death and resurrection of Jesus Christ. As followers of Christ, we believe that Christ Jesus calls us to bear each other's burden and practice solidarity in a world of greed, conflict and division.

We believe in the power of the Holy Spirit, who enables us to discern and act in the right way. In a world where money and profit-driven economic order have become the chief deciding factor for individuals, Christian groups and nations, we reaffirm our belief that the Spirit of Truth should guide every step of the Christian community. (John 16:13-15)

CELEBRATING THE GIFTS OF ADIVASI AND TRIBAL PEOPLE *(While remaining standing)*

Leader:	We celebrate the Tribal and Adivasi symbols of life: "Jal" (water), "Jungle" (forest) and "Jamin" (land).
All:	**May the Tribal and Adivasi communities inspire and lead us in the healing of planet earth that is in deep crisis today.**

Female: Let us celebrate the serenity, simplicity and resilience that many Tribal women exhibit amidst pain and social hopelessness.

All: **We value the Tribal women's wisdom of survival in today's stressful and confusing digital culture.**

Youth: We affirm the drums, dances, folklores and many forms of art that give life and expression to the cultures of Indigenous peoples.

All: **May these symbolic resources allow Indigenous communities to resist prophetically and weave their dreams.**

Male: You toil hard day and night; you are treated as an object; you are dispossessed and evacuated from your dwelling any time of the day. But you amaze me as you continue to serve humanity with faithfulness.

All: **May your hard labour and the social suffering that you undergo bear good fruit through your children and communities.**

Elder: We adore the fresh air of the wild forests and the innocent healing sounds of the brooks that are inhabited by the Adivasi and Indigenous peoples.

All: **May those living in towns and cities appreciate the healing value of fresh air and water.**

INTERCESSION

Leader: Prayer is essential at a time like this. Pray hard. Pray for your sisters and brothers. Keep your eyes open. Keep each other's spirit up so that no one falls behind or drops out.

Elder:	We are deeply pained by the experiences of demoralisation that the Tribal and Adivasi people are undergoing due to the negation of their cultures and identities. We cry out against the different forms of structural, symbolic and physical violence that the minority populations in the nation are undergoing. We are alarmed by the various kinds of social profiling.
All:	**Lord, hear our prayers.**
Male Youth:	We are distressed about the extreme harassment, violence and death that many Indigenous citizens face under the cruel military and police forces. It pains us to see that victims of military and state violence are left with no legal recourse as the perpetrators enjoy legal impunity.
All:	**Lord, hear our prayers.**

Female Youth OR a Community Leader:

We lament for the fast-disappearing art forms and cultural practices of the Indigenous people, and the communitarian values of sharing resources for harmonious coexistence with people and nature that contribute to the richness of community building.

All: **Lord, hear our prayers.**

Male Youth OR a Government Servant:

We are dismayed by the structures and policies that push many Tribal people into poverty, suicide, prostitution and political confrontation.

All: **Lord, hear our prayers.**

Woman OR a Community-Based Organiser:

We mourn for our inaction in the context of the ill health, and loss of livelihood and food security of Indigenous people, caused by displacement, shifts in patterns of cultivation, deforestation, and the use of genetically modified plants.

All: **Lord, hear our prayers**

Man: We pray for freedom of worship, and respect for religious sentiments and sacred places. We are saddened by our inability to exercise the Christian calling of social justice and service in the secular world.

All: **Lord, hear our prayers.**

ACT OF COMMITMENT AS AN EXPRESSION OF SYMBOLIC SOLIDARITY

Symbols may be placed in the centre of the worship place or passed around after the act of every symbolic expression

1.   *Symbol of Hunger/Sustenance:* **Rice, millet, ragi, vegetables,** *etc. (Use an item that is meaningful in your context).*

Leader: Hunger and poverty in a world of market-driven abundance is an insult to God's creation.

Then the leader places or passes the symbol of sustenance in a basket to the congregation.

All: **We are here, creator God; use us as Your instruments to bring abundance to the**

poverty-stricken Adivasi communities, to the landless Tribals, and to the needy Indigenous peoples. We renew our commitment to share with the Adivasi communities joyfully and to guard ourselves against indulgence in greed and luxury.

2.   *Symbol of Injustice/Dignity: Cultural attire, piece of cloth (or any relevant item)*

Leader: Here I stand, my sisters and brothers being dehumanised, treated indifferently, vandalised, murdered, abused, molested. What a pity! What a shame!

To my subjugated Adivasi widow mother, to my alienated Indigenous friend.

To my landless Tribal farmer sister, to my uprooted Tribal father.

I look and stare with foolishness.

For, I am selfish and insecure.

Then the leader places or passes the symbol of dignity in a basket to the congregation.

All: **We are here, weeping God, with sorrow, with wounded and broken hearts. Let us be Your channel of love, Your angel of mercy and messenger of hope, for this is the time for the fullness of life for all. Empower us to work for the dignity of the Indigenous peoples.**

3.   *Symbol of Violence/Peace: Flowers (or any other item symbolising peace)*

Leader: It's deafening, the silence of the oppressed Tribal. I hear people living under constant threat and fear of the military forces. I see divisions and conflicts among Indigenous tribes and ethnic groups. I see corrupt leaders, broken institutions and dying communities in Indigenous societies.

Then the leader places or passes the symbol of dignity in a basket to the congregation.

All: **Here we are, Lord. We humble ourselves before You. We come to renew our minds, our hearts, our souls towards a better understanding of the plight and struggles of our fellow Adivasi, Tribal and Indigenous friends. Give us the strength to carry each other's cross as we journey together in Christ.**

CLOSING SONG

A suitable bhajan or a song that is relevant to your local context can be used.

I, the Lord of sea and sky[3]
I have heard my people cry
All who dwell in dark and sin
My hand will save

I who made the stars of night
I will make their darkness bright
Who will bear my light to them?
Whom shall I send?

---

[3] By Daniel L. Shutte

Chorus   Here I am Lord
                  It is I Lord
                  I have heard You
                  Calling in the night
                  I will go Lord
                  If You lead me
                  I will hold Your people
                  In my heart

I the Lord of snow and rain
I have borne My people's pain
I have wept for love of them
They turn away

I will break their hearts of stone
Give them hearts for love alone
I will speak My word to them
Whom shall I send?   **Chorus**

I the Lord of wind and flame
I will tend the poor and lame
I will set a feast for them
My hand will save

Finest bread I will provide
till their hearts be satisfied
I will give my Life to them
Whom shall I send?   **Chorus**

BENEDICTION

Return to your families, communities and workplaces

And reveal God's saving Spirit through the quality of your life

Dance the goodnews and sound the drum of solidarity

Heal, walk together, bearing one another's burden of body and spirit

In good times and in bad times, commit to living for the glory of God.

References

Miriam Therese Winter, *Woman Word: A Feminist Lectionary and Psalter* (New York, NY: Crossroad, 1990).

National Council of Churches in India *National Policy Guidelines on Indigenous Peoples in India*, Commission on Tribals and Adivasis (Nagpur: NCCI, 2012)

SCMI Song Book, North East India and Jharkand-Bihar Regions (Bangalore: SCMI, 2002)

School of Ecumenical Leadership Formation-2001 (Hong Kong: CCA & WSCF, 2002)

Time for Fullness of Life for All. Asia Youth Week 2000 (Hong Kong: CCA, EGY, 2000)

Your Will Be Done (Singapore: CCA Youth, 1984)

10

From Sanctuary to Street[1]

PRELUDE: *Parai Aattam*[2]

PROCESSIONAL HYMN[3]

The congregation stands for the singing of the processional hymn. While the hymn is being sung, the graduating students, members of the faculty and members of the United Theological College Society enter along with the Chief Guest in procession and take their respective seats.

Great is Your faithfulness, O God Creator,

With You no shadow of turning we see,

You do not change, Your compassions they fail not;

All of Your goodness for ever will be.

---

[1] *This liturgy, contributed by George Zachariah, was used during the Valedictory Service held at the United Theological College in 2015.*

[2] Parai Attam is a subaltern art form, dancing to the beats of *Parai*, a circular wooden frame with one end closed with cow skin membrane and the other end open. It is performed in dances, funerals, temple festivals, sport events, and also to invoke deities.

[3] Text by Thomas O. Chisholm; Music by William M. Runiyan

Chorus   Great is Your faithfulness! Great is Your faithfulness!
Morning by morning new mercies I see;
All I have needed Your hand has provided,
Great is Your faithfulness, God, unto me!

Summer and winter, and springtime and harvest,
Sun, moon, and stars in their courses above,
Join with all nature in manifold witness
To Your great faithfulness, mercy, and love. **Chorus**

Pardon for sin and a peace so enduring,
Your own dear presence to cheer and to guide;
Strength for today and bright hope for tomorrow,
Blessings all mine with ten thousand beside. **Chorus**

OPENING PRAYER

O God of endings and beginnings, O God who transforms endings into beginnings,
O God who sees us as we are and as we are yet to become.
We enter Your presence with great joy to celebrate endings and beginnings.

We offer You every scribbled note and hurried keystroke
Every digested and undigested reading assignment
Every creative and compelling and, yes, rebellious thought
Every deeply troubling conversation, every timely word of comfort and hope
Every sacred element that has defined our life together
As a transforming experience for those who graduate today.

We thank You for Your grace-filled voice
That first called us together and soon calls us apart

In this moment, challenge us and inspire us
Remind us that this celebration
This ending is at the same time a new beginning
For You are not finished with us yet, and You will not let us rest
Until this world truly reflects Your vision of what we are and
who we can be

And so, we offer ourselves in this gathering at this time
To Your transforming love
In Christ's name, **Amen.**

BHAJAN[4]

Yesuvina Namadhali Bhajane Maduve
Nasukinalu Udhayadhalu
Hasivinalu Harasuvenu

Dheenaralli Dheenanathe
Dhalitharali Dahlithananthe
Heenaralli Heenanathe
Dhareglidhu Bandhavanu
Maanavathe Maanavage
Needalendhu Bandhavanu

Badavarige Shubhasamaya
Kurudarige Ravikirana

---

[4] Text and Music: Samson Prabhakar

Bidugadeya aartheyannu
Pasarisalu Bandhavanu
Adigeragi Namisuvenu
Adeevarnu Bhajisuvenu

(Meaning: I praise the name of Christ. In the morning I adore His name. I hunger too, I praise His name. He is the poor among the poorest; the Dalit among the most oppressed; the cast out one among the outcast. He has come to give dignity to humans. He has come to give the poor a good life, the blind, a ray of hope. He has come to spread the message of liberation. We prostrate ourselves and worship the Lord.)

THANKSGIVING *(Modified version of the Magnificat)*
For You take notice of the unnoticeable,
and transform them into the blessed;
You are strong and true to Yourself and all that is good
in everything You are and do and say;
and You do great things for us;
Bless the Lord, my soul, and bless God's holy name.
Bless the Lord, my soul, who leads me into life.

Through the ages, You have shown compassion
to those who trust You,
And in Your strength, You have scattered
those who are arrogant and abusive;
Bless the Lord, my soul, and bless God's holy name.
Bless the Lord, my soul, who leads me into life.

You have made the thrones of tyrants topple

and You have made humble people into leaders of many;
You have cared for and provided for those who have nothing,
and You have left the over-satisfied with empty hands;
Bless the Lord, my soul, and bless God's holy name.
Bless the Lord, my soul, who leads me into life.

You have always been a help to Your people,
and have shown mercy when we have gone astray;
You made this promise to our ancestors,
and You continue to stay true to it even now.
Bless the Lord, my soul, and bless God's holy name.
Bless the Lord, my soul, who leads me into life.

HELP US JESUS: A PRAYER OF CONFESSION

This following is hard, Jesus;
We thought it would be easier somehow;
We didn't count on all the direction and obedience;
We didn't know that Your vineyard would be
where the work would be done
We didn't understand that the benefits would be
for Your kingdom.

But we are learning.
And we see the need more than ever:
The poor who need someone to bring them the good news,
The good news of food, shelter, and sanitation;
The broken who need a healer to comfort them, and guide
them to wholeness;
The oppressed and imprisoned who need justice and freedom,

from the bonds that hold them;

The excluded and the demonised, who lack respect, voice, identity, and freedom to be different;

The powerful who need prophets to call them to account and call out the best within them;

The earth, which needs earth-healing communities to nurture, protect, and celebrate life.

Jesus, we need courage and humility to stay faithful to Your purpose;

To give our best, not for our own sake, but Yours—and that of those You love;

To labour in Your vineyard, to let the world experience Your transforming grace and love, Amen.

CONGREGATIONAL HYMN[5]

(As we sing this song, offertory shall be brought forward.)

Christ is all to me, Jesus Christ is all to me
In this world of strife and sorrow, Christ is all to me

Brother He, me brother calls; Bridegroom He, the Church His bride;
Parent, Kinsman, Master, Saviour; And to each His Friend and Guide.

Watching me with shepherd-care; Lovingly my wants attends,
My companion all the way till evening falls and journey ends.

Peace when storms around me blow, joy in sorrow, calm in strife,

---

[5] Text by D. T. Niles; Music by Adaikalam A. Gnanadoss

Health in sickness, wealth in want, the noonday sun, the light
of life.

Teacher of the truth of God, Prophet of God's heavenly reign,
Sent of God that we may find in Serving Him eternal gain.

He the prize and He the goal and by Him the race begun,
He the runner of the team who will complete the race I run.

SCRIPTURE READING

SERMON   From Sanctuary to Street

COMMITMENT SONG[6]
Jesus Christ is waiting,
Waiting in the streets;
No one is His neighbour,
All alone He eats.
Listen, Lord Jesus,
I am lonely too.
Make me, friend or stranger,
Fit to wait on You

Jesus Christ is raging,
Raging in the streets,
Where injustice spirals
And real hope retreats.
Listen, Lord Jesus,
I am angry too.

---

[6] Text & Music: Iona Community: John L. Bell and Graham Maule

In the Kingdom's causes
Let me rage with You.

Jesus Christ is healing,
Healing in the streets;
Curing those who suffer,
Touching those He greets.
Listen, Lord Jesus,
I have pity too.
Let my care be active,
Healing just like You.

Jesus Christ is dancing,
Dancing in the streets,
Where each sign of hatred
He, with love, defeats.
Listen, Lord Jesus,
I should triumph too.
On suspicion's graveyard
Let me dance with You.

Jesus Christ is calling,
Calling in the streets,
"Who will join my journey?
I will guide their feet."
Listen, Lord Jesus,
Let my fears be few.

Walk one step before me;
I will follow You.

FROM SANCTUARY TO STREET: A PRAYER OF COMMITMENT BY THE GRADUATING STUDENTS

Here in this sanctuary,
we remember, O God, Your gift of life to each of us;
and we seek to carry it to the streets—
wherever there is death and violence
wherever there is grief and loss.

Here in this sanctuary,
we remember, O God, Your invitation to belong and find shelter;
and we seek to carry it to the streets—
wherever there is loneliness and rejection
wherever there is homelessness and people are displaced.

Here in this sanctuary,
we remember, O God, Your reign of justice and righteousness;
and we seek to carry it to the streets—
wherever there is lawlessness or tyranny
wherever there is corruption and oppression.

Here in this sanctuary,
we remember, O God, Your sacrifice of love and mercy;
and we seek to carry it to the streets—
wherever there is hatred and evil
wherever there is hopelessness, regret and guilt.

Here in this sanctuary, where we remember all that You have done for us, O God,

we remember also Your call to live what we sing and pray.

And so we commit ourselves again

to carry our ministry from the sanctuary to the streets.

In Jesus' Name, **Amen.**

LITANY OF COMMISSIONING

Leader: You have waited patiently for the Lord and the Lord has heard your cry.
He has called you to be His servants and He keeps you and blesses you as you go out into the world to serve Him.

Congregation: The Lord has lifted you and drawn you out of the desolate pit.
He inspired you when you needed inspiration;
gave you rest when you needed sleep;
helped you find answers when you had questions.
Strengthened you to ask the right questions to contest easy answers
He delivered you from the hard slog of "Christian Tradition"
and the ramblings of dead theologies.

Graduating Students: You have multiplied, O Lord,
Your wondrous deeds and thoughts towards us;

Just as You blessed our studies, You will bless our ministries
as we embody in the world, our hope of Christ's return.

Leader: Happy are those who trust in the Lord,
who pick up their cross and follow Jesus.
Happy are those who do not become proud,
and chase after the false gods of this age.

Graduating Students: God, You have put a new song into our mouths,
a song of praise to You.
May the world know that You sent us
by the song of Your love in our lives.

All: **We have waited patiently for the Lord and the Lord heard our cry.**
We are the people of God, shaped and moulded by the story of God, freed from our sins by the life of Christ, who anointed us as His disciples.
The Lord has called us to be His servants and He will keep us and bless us as we go into the world to serve Him.

PRAYERS OF THE PEOPLE

Confident in the gracious and ever-widening mercy of God,

Let us pray for the world, the body of Christ, and all who yearn for the wholeness of life.

Liberate us from our bondage to sin, God of freedom, that Your Church would continually be reshaped and reformed by the fire of the Holy Spirit.

O Lord, hear our prayer, O Lord, hear our prayer when we call answer us

O Lord, hear our prayer, O Lord, hear our prayer, come and listen to us.

Show your righteousness, God of justice, that all who are oppressed and marginalised, forgotten, and discriminated against, would affirm their voice and identity, and reclaim their right to live with dignity.

O Lord, hear our prayer, O Lord, hear our prayer when we call answer us

O Lord, hear our prayer, O Lord, hear our prayer, come and listen to us.

Take us by our hand, God of companionship, when we are paralysed by our fears and unable to step out in boldness. Give us the courage to walk confidently with you.

O Lord, hear our prayer, O Lord, hear our prayer when we call answer us

O Lord, hear our prayer, O Lord, hear our prayer, come and listen to us.

Give your stillness, God of calm, to all who are facing illness, surgery, or any uncertainty of health. May they know that their times are in Your ever-healing hands.

O Lord, hear our prayer, O Lord, hear our prayer when we call answer us

O Lord, hear our prayer, O Lord, hear our prayer, come and listen to us.

We pray for the United Theological College and its mission and ministry to equip the saints for Your ministry. Enable us to stay focused on our call, and to serve You without considering the cost. We pray for the UTC Community, past and present, the Churches, ecumenical bodies, social action groups, social movements, and all our partners. Give us the discernment to engage in doing theology, discerning the signs of the times.

O Lord, hear our prayer, O Lord, hear our prayer when we call answer us

O Lord, hear our prayer, O Lord, hear our prayer, come and listen to us.

Listen to us when we call upon You, most merciful God, and grant us grace to entrust our lives and our world to your unfailing love, through Christ our Lord. **Amen.**

CLOSING HYMN[7]

We are marching in the light of God
We are dancing in the light of God
We are singing in the light of God
We are praying in the light of God

---

[7] South African Freedom Song

THE LORD'S PRAYER (In vernacular)

SENDING[8]

May God bless you with discomfort
At easy answers, half-truths, and superficial relationships,
So that you may live deep within your heart.

May God bless you with anger
At injustice, oppression and exploitation of people,
So that you may work for justice, freedom and peace.

May God bless you with tears
To shed for those who suffer pain, rejection, hunger, and war,
So that you may reach out your hand to comfort them
And turn their pain into joy.

And may God bless you with enough foolishness
To believe that you can make a difference in the world,
So that you can do what others claim cannot be done
To bring justice and kindness to all our children and the poor.
Amen

CHORAL BENEDICTION[9]

The Lord bless you and keep you
The Lord lift his countenance upon you, and give you peace
The Lord make his face to shine upon you, and be gracious
unto you, **Amen.**

---

[8] A Franciscan Blessing

[9] Composed by Peter C. Lutkin

POSTLUDE

While the Parai Aattam is being performed, the recession of the members of the United Theological Community Society, members of the faculty, Senior Administrative Staff and the graduates start. The congregation may greet the graduates, who will form a semicircle in the lawn close to the college entrance.

ACKNOWLEDGMENT

Taize Community

www.sacredise.com

www.lovegrowshere.org

www.ptstulsa.edu

www.mennodiscuss.com

11

Hope for a New Spirituality[1]

CALL TO WORSHIP *(All seated)*

In a time of war, to pray for peace

In a time of injustice, to pray for justice

In a time of fear, to pray for courage

In a time of despair, to pray for hope

In a time of action, as a sign of faith

In a time of darkness, as a sign of light

We have chosen to be here

As one in the Spirit; Yes, we are one in Christ.

OPENING PRAYER *(All standing)*

As bruised reeds, feeble and fickle, we come

Make us stable, O Lord.

As burning wicks, faint and flickering, we come

Kindle us ablaze, O Lord.

---

[1] *A liturgy prepared by Viji Varghese Eapen, for CWM South Asia Regional Assembly 2018*

In unison: You are our hope; "Hope for Renewal", "Hope for a New Spirituality" and "Hope for Tomorrow". Amen.

OPENING HYMN[2]

To God be the glory, great things He hath done,
So loved He the world that He gave us His Son,
Who yielded His life our redemption to win,
And opened the life-gate that all may go in.

Chorus   Praise the Lord, praise the Lord,
                   Let the earth hear His voice;
                   Praise the Lord, praise the Lord,
                   Let the people rejoice;
                   Oh, come to the Father, through Jesus the Son,
                   And give Him the glory; great things He hath
                   done.

Oh, perfect redemption, the purchase of blood,
To every believer the promise of God;
The vilest offender who truly believes,
That moment from Jesus a pardon receives.

Great things He hath taught us, great things He hath done,
And great our rejoicing through Jesus the Son;
But purer, and higher, and greater will be
Our wonder, our transport when Jesus we see.

Kindly be seated

---

[2] Text by Fanny Crosby; Music by Howard Doane.

CONFESSION

In our nations and Churches in South Asia, for failing to realise that there are no bounds to Your capacity for love,

Silence

Merciful God,
Forgive us. Correct us. Lead us.

In our nations and Churches in South Asia, for not living as communicators of Your inclusive love for all creations,

Silence

Merciful God,
Forgive us. Correct us. Lead us.

In our nations and Churches in South Asia, for our reluctance to live as Your arms and voices, engaging in the extension of Your realm,

Silence

Merciful God,
Forgive us. Correct us. Lead us.

In our nations and Churches in South Asia, for refraining ourselves from Your call to be co-creators,

Silence

Merciful God,
Forgive us. Correct us. Lead us.

In our nations and Churches in South Asia, for exploiting the earth, resulting in drastic climate change, global warming and environmental hazards,

Silence

Merciful God,

Forgive us. Correct us. Lead us.

In our nations and Churches in South Asia, for not voicing to speak for those Indigenous communities who are silenced,

Silence

Merciful God,

Forgive us. Correct us. Lead us.

In our nations and Churches in South Asia, for being dormant in restoring the displaced, in feeding the hungry, in visiting the sick and comforting the faint-hearted,

Silence

Merciful God,

Forgive us. Correct us. Lead us.

ABSOLUTION

For preferring to stay where we are and for being comfortable in our spaces,

For being obsessed with our prejudices and for being reluctant to reach others,

For being unwilling to preach Your love, Forgive us O Lord.

Now may You transform us and lead us towards a New Spirituality. **Amen.**

SCRIPTURE READING   2 Kings 6: 13-23

SERMON   Hope for a New Spirituality

HYMN *(All standing)*[3]

No more we live in world of peace,
No more we have a breathing space.
Valley of bones we see around,
Craving to live and move around.

Chorus   Our hope is built on Christ, the Peace
                All other ground is sinking sand;
                All other ground is sinking sand.

Our people long for days of peace
Our people cry for Your justice
Speak to us, God, now speak to us
Speak through us, God, now speak through us.   **Chorus**

Come let us beat our swords to plows
And beat our spears to pruning hooks
To lift the world from groaning days,
To wipe the tears from mourning face.   **Chorus**

Kindly be seated.

SERMON

AFFIRMATION OF FAITH *(All standing)*

We believe in You, who dwells within and loves everything in
the whole universe.

We believe in You, the Creator.

---

[3] Set to the tune of the Hymn "My Hope is Built on Nothing Less," text
by Edward Mote; music by William B. Bradbury)

We believe in You, who calls us to affirm the rights of those who are denied life.
We believe in You, the Redeemer.

We believe in You, who guides us to impart hope by caring for the people and healing the nations.
We believe in You, the Sustainer.

God, this world of diverse views, religious orientations and cultural differences,
We believe, is Your creation.

God, to proclaim the good news of hope through love, peace and justice,
We believe, is Your mission.

God, Your Church who is called to witness Your all-encompassing love,
We believe, is Your Body.

In Unison: **We believe,**
               You are with us, in our pains and glory
               You are with us in life, in death and life beyond life,
               This be our hope, this be our spirituality, forever and ever. Amen.

PRAYERS OF INTERCESSION[4] (*All seated*)

God, we pray for those in South Asia, who are poor, who are

---

[4] A different form of this same prayer is used in another liturgy, 'A Liturgy of Worship for/by the Youth' published in this book.

reduced to poverty and suffering due to debts, genocides, rapes, human trafficking and communal violence.

Silence

Blessed are the poor in spirit, for theirs is the kingdom of God.

God, we pray for those in South Asia, who are victims of wars, internal conflicts and violence.

Silence

Blessed are they who mourn, for they shall be comforted.

God, we pray for those in South Asia who are denied livelihood and food, and are persecuted, tortured and massacred because they are Dalits and Tribals or Adivasis.

Silence

Blessed are those who hunger and thirst for righteousness' sake, for they will be filled.

God, we pray for our Churches in South Asia where the rich and affluent are more visible and heard, where there are marked disparities among the dioceses and congregations.

Silence

Blessed are the merciful, for they will receive mercy.

God, we pray for the Council for World Mission, all its member Churches and their leaders, that with a good heart and a pure conscience they may accomplish Your ministry.

Silence

Blessed are the pure in heart, for they will see God.

God, we pray for South Asia, especially for Bangladesh, our host nation, particularly for those who struggle for their freedom, expression and identity.

Silence

Blessed are those who are persecuted for righteousness sake, for theirs is the kingdom of heaven.

God, we pray for all those who confess the name of Christ, especially for those who are persecuted, as they engage in acts of justice and peace, as Your disciples.

Silence

Blessed are you when people revile you and persecute you and utter all kinds of evil against you falsely on my account.

In unison: Let us rejoice and be glad, for it is said, 'Your reward is great in heaven.' Grant us this grace, O God. Amen.

Let us pray the Lord's Prayer in our native language/vernacular

CLOSING HYMN[5] *(All standing)*
O God, our help in ages past,
Our hope for years to come,
Our shelter from the stormy blast,
And our eternal home.

Under the shadow of Thy throne
Thy saints have dwelt secure;

---

[5] Text by Isaac Watts and Music attributed to William Croft

Sufficient is Thine arm alone,
And our defence is sure.

Before the hills in order stood,
Or earth received her frame,
From everlasting Thou art God,
To endless years the same.

A thousand ages in Thy sight
Are like an evening gone;
Short as the watch that ends the night
Before the rising sun.

Time, like an ever-rolling stream,
Bears all its sons away;
They fly forgotten, as a dream
Dies at the opening day.

O God, our help in ages past,
Our hope for years to come,
Be Thou our guard while life shall last,
And our eternal home.

BENEDICTION

May we depart from this place and time, to be a voice of peace
in a time of conflict, a voice of justice in a time of oppression,
a voice of love in a time of callousness. May the God of Peace,
Justice and Love bless us and sustain us in our journey towards
a New Spirituality. **Amen.**

12

Globalisation and Youth[1]

Hi everybody,

Good Morning!

Its time for us to "log in";

Not just to have a "chat" with Him, not just to "like" His "status", not just to "comment" on His "posts",

But to get connected and remain connected with Him, our Creator, Redeemer and Sustainer.

Come, let us "google" the depth of His love and "follow" His statutes.

Let us pray:

O God, who has set our "templates" and "timelines," today we come to You as youth gathered together from various

---

[1] *This liturgy, prepared by Viji Varghese Eapen, was used during the Inaugural Worship of the 'FEST-ZOE:2012' (International Ecumenical Youth Consultation on "Globalization & Youth Culture") held at the CSI Synod, Chennai, during 12–17 November 2012.*

corners of Your world. We praise You, for, Your gigabytes are uncountable, Your computing power inconceivable. We come as nothing before You, and without You, we are nothing. May we through this worship, experience Your grace so that we see You face to face and rejoice in peace. We pray this in the mighty name of our Lord and Saviour Jesus Christ. **Amen.**

Let us all stand and sing the hymn[2]
Be glad in the Lord, and rejoice,
All ye that are upright in heart;
And ye that have made Him your choice,
Bid sadness and sorrow depart.

Chorus
Rejoice, rejoice,
Be glad in the Lord and rejoice;
Rejoice, rejoice,
Be glad in the Lord and rejoice

Be joyful, for He is the Lord,
On earth and in Heaven supreme;
He fashions and rules by His word—
The 'Mighty' and 'Strong' to redeem.

What though in the conflict for right
Your enemies almost prevail?
God's armies, just hid from your sight,
Are more than the foes which assail.

Though darkness surround you by day,
Your sky by the night be o'ercast,

---

[2] Text by Mary E. Servoss; Music by James Mc Granahan

Let nothing your spirit dismay,
But trust till the danger is past.

Be glad in the Lord, and rejoice,
His praises proclaiming in song;
With harp and with organ and voice
The loud hallelujahs prolong!
Let us all be seated and "browse" ourselves in silence:
While millions around us were crying for help, we often chose to remain busy wearing headphones and listening to the latest hits. We failed in loving others.

Silence

God,

Help us to quarantine the virus of "indifference" within us.

While millions around us were craving for food and water, we often chose to remain away from them, enjoying and partying day and night. We failed in loving others.
Silence

God,

Help us to quarantine the virus of "selfishness" within us.

While millions around us were struggling in poverty, we often chose to remain in our own cellars, praying for our own prosperity. We failed in loving others.
Silence

God,

Help us to quarantine the virus of "materialism" within us.

While millions around us were suffering due to ecological catastrophes, we often chose to remain in front of our TVs, watching those moments and passing judgements. We failed in loving others.

Silence

God,

Help us to quarantine the virus of "self-righteousness" within us.

While millions around us were being sexually assaulted, we often chose to "forward" those as MMS and "share" those as videos. We failed in loving others.

Silence

God,

Help us to quarantine the virus of "hedonism" within us.

God, we confess that we have often walked through the valleys of "spam" and "malwares." We confess that we have often opted for "pirated" ethos and values and have become "corrupted." We pray that You "scan" us, "format" us, and "re-install" Your image within us, so that we love You with a whole heart and love each other as we love ourselves. In Jesus name we pray, **Amen.**

As we remain seated, let us listen to the Scripture Reading 1 Corinthians 13: 1-7

1.   f I spk n d tungs of mrtls n of angls, bt dnt av lov, ima nocy gong or a clngng cmbal.

2.   n f Ive prophetic pwrs, n undrst& ll X-files n ll nolage, n f Ive ll fath, so as 2 rmv ^v^v^, bt dnt av lov, im Ø.

3.   f I giv awy ll my Blngngs, n f I h& ovr my bod so dat I may bost, bt dnt av lov, I gain Ø.

4.   lov S patient; lov S knd; lov aint nVS or boastful or argnt.

5.   or rude. It duznt nsist on its on wa; itz nt iritbl or rsntfl;

6.   it duznt rjc n wrongdoing, bt rjcs n d trth.

7.   It bers ll thngs, Blevz ll thngs, hps ll thngs, ndrs ll thngs.

Let us all stand and sing together[3]:

As we worship, now You, O Lord
One who made world through Word
One who called us to spread the Word
Bless us with Spirit poured.

Youth, we come to Your feet, O Lord
To further peace in world
Now may we hear and taste Your Word
And by Your Spirit, filled.

Young men and women, we come Lord
May You melt us and mould
Through the thick and the thin, we tread
May our hands, You do hold.

---

[3] Text by Viji Varghese Eapen, set to the tune of "Jesus, the very thought of Thee," text by (attributed to) Bernard of Clairvaux (translator: Edward Caswal) and tune: *St. Agnes*, composed by John Bacchus Dykes

As we prepare to march forward
You be our friend and guide
Let we be always on Your side
And with the poor we side.
May we all be seated and listen to the 'Homily'

Homily: Globalisation & Youth Culture

Kindly be seated and let us pray.[4]

We live in a world where mountains of garbage pile up, nuclear waste threaten life, where trees are cut down at a fatally faster rate.

Gd, trn our :'-(n2 :-)) *[God turn our mourning into rejoicing]*

God, "untag" us from the culture of exploitation.

We live in a world were 20% have more food than what they need, while 80% go hungry.
Gd, trn our :'-(n2 :-))

God, "untag" us from the culture of accumulation.

We live in a world where many are reduced to poverty suffering due to debts, genocides, rapes, human trafficking and communal violence.
Gd, trn our :'-(n2 :-))

God, "untag" us from the culture of violence.

We live in a world where large sections of people are denied livelihood and food, simply because they are Dalits and

---

[4] A different form of this same prayer is used in another liturgy composed by me. See, 'A Liturgy for the CWM South Asia Region Regional Assembly' published in this book.

Tribals or Adivasis.

Gd, trn our :'-(n2 :-))

God, "untag" us from the culture of injustice.

In our Churches often the rich and affluent are more visible and heard, where there are marked disparities among the dioceses and congregations.

Gd, trn our :'-(n2 :-))

God, "untag" us from the culture of discrimination.

In our Churches, often a few become stronger by the day and the people on the margins are pushed to anonymity.

Gd, trn our :'-(n2 :-))

God, "untag" us from the culture of oppression.

In our Churches growth is understood only in terms of Church membership and bank accounts, and the poor and the weaker sections often fail to be recognised

Gd, trn our :'-(n2 :-))

God, "untag" us from the culture of materialism.

Let us pray the Lord's Prayer in our respective mother tongue

Let us say the benediction in unison:
As we "sign out", may the Triune God help us to remain "logged in." Let us continue to "upload" our concerns, "download" His will and "share" His love and compassion. Let our "folders" and "files" be filled by His words and thoughts. Let us "subscribe" to His "pages." And now may the Grace, Love and Peace of the Triune God "follow" us all through this camp. Amen.

———————

LITURGICAL RESOURCES

1

Call to Worship at COVID Times[1]

Although COVID limits our chances of celebrating Eucharist as a sacrament within a sanctuary, it cannot stop us from enjoying the Eucharist as a communion present at all times and at all places. When we are distressed and anguished, the Lord invites us to this restoring fellowship.

Under the solitary broom tree, I sit and pray,
"It is enough; now, O Lord, take away my life."
"Get up and eat."
Alone, we suffer.
"Come to me, I will give you rest."

At the shore of Galilee, besides the charcoal fire,
With fish on it, and bread, He invites,
"Come and have breakfast."
Confused, we wait.
"Come to me, I will give you rest."

---

[1] *By Viji Varghese Eapen*

At Emmaus, He sat down at table, blessed the bread and broke it,
And gave it to us, saying,
"Take. Eat."
Shaken, we grieve.
"Come to me, I will give you rest."

———————————

2

Opening Prayer and Confession[1]

Creator God, we thank You for Your manifestations through people, places and situations. We believe that your revelation is not limited to the Scripture we adhere to but freely overflows into the locations that are detestable and to people who await You. Your dialogue with the first earthlings dilutes the disparities that separate us. Your oneness with Your creation invites us to perceive You as one among us, listening, walking, conversing, responding to our cries and participating in our joys. We come before You leaving behind our prejudices against people, their religious backgrounds, their denominational difference, their caste identity, their physical ability, their sexual expression, biological difference and their age difference. We all come as one people waiting to experience Your revelation in one another. In Jesus name, we pray. **Amen.**

God in diverse forms, we confess that our attitudes have distorted Your image in us. Our prejudices have severed the sincerity in our relationships. We have often been the yardstick

---

[1] *By S. Helen Chukka*

to judge our neighbour's religion, caste, sex, ability and the like. Our faith expressions have been hurtful to people of different faiths. Our complacency has disrupted the trust our fellow human beings had in us. Enable us to realise that our silence is dangerous. Renew within us a spirit of reconciliation so that we may engage in a radical reconciliation that corrects the wrongs and may our actions instil trust in those who have lost it. May our lives be transformed by Your liberating spirit and help us to work towards eradicating the boundaries we continue to create. Forgive us for our negligence in participating to be a sanctuary community where all are welcome irrespective of who we are.

If we say we have no sin, we deceive ourselves, but if confess our sins and acknowledge our shortcomings in overcoming our sins, God makes God-self available to us to fill us with God's spirit that renews us and imparts in us the Spirit of Love that transcends all barriers.

———————————

3

A Confession Liturgy for the Medical Fraternity[1]

Have we not heard of him with leprosy, who came to Jesus for healing? Jesus was filled with compassion. He touched the leper and made him whole.

Are we quick in judging and slow in loving our sisters and brothers who suffer from the stigma more than the disease itself, especially those living with HIV and AIDS?

Silence

Forgive us and heal us, O Lord.

Have we not heard of her, suffering due to bleeding for 12 years, who touched Jesus' garment for healing? Healing power went out of Jesus and allowed her to be healed.

Are we not sometimes profit-oriented, failing to offer medical services to the poor and the marginalised around us?

Silence

---

[1] *By Viji Varghese Eapen*

Forgive us and heal us, O Lord.

Have we not heard of him who was sick for 38 years with no one to help him to get into the pond and healed, looking to Jesus for healing? Jesus showed him compassion and healed him.

Are we not sometimes unkind and impatient with those who are terminally ill, considering them a burden?

Silence

Forgive us and heal us, O Lord.

Have we not heard of the four men who carried a paralytic in a bed and let him down right in the middle of the crowd where Jesus was, for healing? Jesus, seeing their faith, healed him.

Are we not sometimes reluctant to offer and create spaces for our sisters and brothers who are differently-abled and mentally challenged, to experience the healing touch of Jesus.

Silence

Forgive us and heal us, O Lord.

In unison   *(Set to the tune of the Hymn "Abide with me")*

Tears, will I wipe as I stretch out my hand
Smiles, will I give as seeds of hope I plant
Fear, shame and questions, all these I impeach
As Christ reached out to me, so will I reach.

———————

Psalm 1:
Rereading from the Dalit Perspective[1]

§ Blessed are the people who do not walk and live in the counsel of the ungodly and inhuman caste system, nor stands in the way of oppressors nor sits in the seat of the scornful oppressive taskmasters of caste.

§ Those people's delight is in the reign of God, whose law is justice, equality and dignity; and in such a law, these people reflect, respond, struggle and strive to establish them here on earth, both day and night.

§ And these people shall be like a tree planted by the rivers of water of justice and righteousness that brings forth their fruits of liberation in all seasons; their leaves shall remain green without drying out, never giving up their concern for libreration; and whatsoever they take up for the cause of Dalit human rights shall bear fruit.

---

[1] *By Raj Bharat Patta*

§ The ungodly, inhuman caste oppressors are not so; but are like the chaff which the wind drives away from the society.

§ Therefore, all those who uphold, preach and practice ungodly and inhuman caste discrimination shall have to go for trial, and the judgement will be very harsh for they cannot withstand; nor will these caste people will have a place in the fellowship and community of the reign of God.

§ For the God of justice knows and leads the way for those seeking liberation, but the way of those people who practise the ungodly and inhuman caste discrimination shall be destined to doom and destruction.

5

Rereading of the Magnificat:
The Canticle of the Virgin Mary (Luke 1: 46-55)[1]

My soul is deeply wounded with hurts, insults and pains
And my spirits are drowning in the floods of sorrows and rains
my soul still glorifies the Lord, seeking justice as all gains
And my spirit rejoices in God my saviour despite my stains
and strains

When I am rejected and discriminated as polluted
People conspired, laughed at me, brought me to public and
collated
For except you, O Lord, none has been mindful
Of me your humble servant to do anything needful

Though all my family members call me cursed
Blaming me that I made the image of our family bruised,

---

[1] *By Raj Bharat Patta*

But there will come a day when all generations call me blessed
For the Mighty One has been doing me great things so impressed.

As a Wonderful Counsellor, God solaced and comforted me
as lovingly Yours
As a Mighty One, God strengthened me with all God's powers
As an Everlasting God, God journeyed with me in my darkest
hours
As Prince of Peace, God encouraged me to win overall conflicting
towers
For holy is God's name and truly victory flowers

When I am surrounded by fear
When I am pushed down to death near
I could only fear God who is so dear
Realising that God's mercy is with me now here
From generations to generations vivid and clear

When several arms geared up to stone me to death,
God's mighty arm guarded me against them above and beneath;
When the proud religious heads gathered to take me for a ride,
God scattered the pride, saving me as his bride

Those that are drunk with power and are lusted with hierarchy,
God will throw down such to their cruelty and anarchy;
God shall lift those who are humble and suffer sinful tyranny
For God shares freedom to both a few and many.

Those that go to bed every day in hunger,
Those that curse the selfish accumulators in anger,
God will fill them with good things satisfying
And sends the rich empty, for God, it's justifying

God has always remembered to be prudent and merciful
Helping all the slaves in history to be liberated in their full
Making all our ancestors be such channels so graceful
Leaving a legacy to carry forward and be fruitful.

(This Magnificat has been reread in juxtaposing two significant contexts. One situating Mother Mary as a young woman, who faced enormous challenges in her society, as she was conceived even before she knew her husband, Joseph. The other is in light of the realities of violence against women, a continuing reality in all histories.)

6

We Believe in God, the Baker of Bread: A Faith Affirmation[1]

We believe in God, the baker of bread,

We believe in God, who bakes bread daily and shares it equally among all people, who are created equally in the image of God,

We believe in God, who spread a table in the wilderness to the people of Israel,

We believe in God, who smote the rock so that water gushed out and stream overflowed,

We believe in God, who rained down upon the people manna to eat for forty years sufficiently,

We believe in God, who gave the people the grain of heaven in abundance,

We believe in God, who fed God's people through creative sources and resources in times of hunger.

---

[1] *By Raj Bharat Patta*

We believe in Jesus Christ, the Son of God the baker of bread,

We believe in Jesus Christ, the bread of life, who has come down from heaven to give life to the world,

We believe in Jesus Christ, who was born in a manger in the little town of the house of bread (Bethlehem) to be in solidarity with all those hungry and people without food,

We believe in Jesus Christ, who taught His disciples to pray, 'Give us today our daily bread', calling all to share our daily bread with those in hunger and need,

We believe in Jesus Christ, who shared food with five thousand people using local recipes like bread and fish, countering the vices of greed, consumerism and globalisation,

We believe in Jesus Christ, the living bread, whose body was broken in saving the entire creation,

We believe in Jesus Christ, who shared His bread to His disciples and pronounced to do the same in remembrance of Him so that they shall not die but be alive,

We believe in Jesus Christ, who as was resurrected from the clutches of deaths, joined His disciples in dining together with them to eat bread and fish, granting a new hope of life,

We believe in Jesus Christ, who shall come to judge the living and the dead by questioning, 'Did you feed the least of my brothers and sisters who were hungry and thirsty?'

We believe in the Holy Spirit, the advocate who fights for the cause of the hungry and people without food,

We believe in the Holy Spirit, the advocate for the rights of food security, food sovereignty and one who intercedes for the right to food for all people,

We believe in the Holy Spirit, the liberating spirit, that helps people of God to be the leaven amidst the flour of creation to make an impact on others to become responsible towards sustainability of food for all,

We believe in the Holy Spirit, who calls all people to join in the Eucharist to share in the common bread and common wine with all people, transcending the barriers of gender, caste, religion and region.

We believe in God, the baker of bread, who grants daily bread to all people.

7

Affirmation of Faith: An Ecological Perspective[1]

I believe in God, the creator of the "Land" the whole universe, the raw material for all that is in this universe.

I believe in Jesus Christ, the universal farmer who had no piece of land to lay his head, conceived by the powerful intervention of the Holy Spirit, born of the Virgin Mary, a woman with a vision. He made the victims speak for themselves, encouraging the marginalised and the subalterns to bring about a reformation in society; with the soil and his saliva, He healed, hence, included the whole creation as active agents in His mission; fed the five thousand with equal and just shares, thus, made justice in the distribution systems ensuring the livelihoods for communities; yet suffered and groaned for the redemption of the whole creation and died. But, on the third day, He rose again as an offspring shoot with new life showing His resiliency, giving hope to the desperate communities.

---

[1] *By Chrisida Anandan*

I believe in the Holy Spirit, who makes us conscious of dehumanising imbalances in the individual and collective relationship; the universal Church that stands in solidarity with the vulnerable ones; the communion of the whole creation as one community of God; the forgiveness of sins for our redemption; the resurrection of the body and life everlasting.

8

An Ecological Intercession[1]

Creator God, we thank you for creating this earth as holy ground. We pray that we recognise that the environment is God's gift to everyone, and in our use of it, we have a responsibility towards the poor, towards future generations and humanity as a whole. Help us to recognise that our grave duty is to hand the earth on to future generations in such a condition that they too can worthily inhabit it and continue to cultivate it. Enable us to defend earth, water and air as gifts of creation that belong to everyone. Commission us to be active advocates for a healthier planet so that we set an excellent example for our children in the way we care for the earth.

Hear our voice, O Lord.

We pray for all farmers, growers, all who tend the livestock and all who by their labour is so close to the land and the earth. Help us to appreciate and recognise them for the awesome responsibility they have in their hands. Bless their endeavours and their crops. May we value their work and be responsible

---

[1] *By Chrisida Anandan*

citizens. We pray for the people and lands that have suffered from natural and human-made disasters, that there is a return to hope and that bountiful resources may help restore the people and the land to wholeness. Grant power of resiliency to the communities so that our relationships and livelihoods are restored with hope.

Hear our prayers, O Lord.

We pray for all the decision-makers to make decisions that will preserve our earth that they may persist and not lose hope. We pray for all non-profit agencies and organisations devoted to the care of the earth. We pray for government officials throughout the world that they may use their influence and power positively to enact and monitor legislation meant to protect the environment.

Hear our prayers, O Lord.

Enable us to take responsibility for our own choices and become educated about how we can effectively contribute to the preservation of the environment. Let us make lifestyle choices that favour the earth. Let us walk with gratitude for receiving this gift of our beautiful world. In Jesus' name, we pray, **Amen.**

9

The Lord's Prayer (Modified)[1]

Our God who is amidst us, Your name will be glorified,
When we promote justice and stand up for equality.

We are in the process of discovering Your Kin-dom,
Which can be realised when the marginal communities cease being marginal.

Give us today the willingness
To discern right from wrong.

Forgive our sins of complacency and silence
Which are hurtful for the oppressed.

Help us to resist our temptation
To exploit power bestowed on us.

---

[1] *By S. Helen Chukka*

But, enable us to be in solidarity
With the marginal communities.

Deliver us, O Lord,
From fascism and narcissism.

May power be distributed to all
And may we experience Your glory. Amen

———————————

10

The Lord's Prayer (Modified)[1]

Our Father/Mother/Parent,
Whose nature is of a circle of which the centre is everywhere,
and the circumference is nowhere,
Hallowed be Your name.

Who exercises the sovereign power upon all the creations through the values of peace, love and justice.
Your reign come.

Help us to develop our powers of body and mind to desire, not superficially, but consciously realising what the cost could be, that Your will be done,
On earth as it is in Heaven.

Who has taught us not to be greedy as those who have more dinners than their appetite but to share with those who have more appetite than their dinners,
Give us this day our daily bread.

---

[1] *By Viji Varghese Eapen*

Who wants us to have a sense of right and wrong, to do only the right things, forgive us for consent to all kinds of wrongs, both open and disguised,
As we forgive those who have failed us.

Help us not to yield to the temptation of doing the right deeds for wrong reasons or wrong deeds for the right reasons,
But, deliver us from evil.

In unison: For Yours is the reign, Yours is the power, and Yours is the glory, forever and ever. Amen.

———————————

11

___

The Lord's Prayer (Eco-Version)[1]

Our Parent in Heaven,
The sole owner of this earth and all that is in it

Let Your name be glorified
Through our lives as agents of justice and peace

May Your reign come
As we inhabit this earth as mere caretakers and not as rulers of dominion

Your will be done on earth as it is in heaven
As we strive hard to ensure that we have resilient livelihoods, communities and relationships

Give us this day our daily bread
To make sure that we will not waste food or accumulate resources so that no one will be left hungry

___

[1] *By Chrisida Anandan*

Forgive our sins

Of perverse inequalities in the distribution of everyday goods and each person's opportunities for development

Lead us not into temptations

As we may tend to compromise with materialism and accretion of vast land holdings, at the expense of others

But deliver us from evil

Of selfish motives and individualism

For Yours is the reign,

Of justice and righteousness

Power,

That provides resilience to the vulnerable communities,

And authority,

Of restoration of hope and liberation with love

Now and forever more, **Amen.**

———————————

12

An Eco-Litany for Commitment[1]

To bring new life to the land, to restore the waters, to refresh the air,
We join with the earth and with each other.

To renew the forests, to care for the plants, to protect the creatures,
We join with the earth and with each other.

To celebrate the seas, to rejoice in the sunlight, to sing the song of the stars,
We join with the earth and with each other.

To recreate the human community, to promote justice and peace, to remember our children,
We join with the earth and with each other.

---

[1] *By Viji Varghese Eapen*

In unison: We join together as many and diverse expressions of one loving mystery: for the healing of the earth and the renewal of life.

Help us, O Lord, to partake in Your mission to be caretakers of Your creation. Amen.

13

An Eco-Blessing[1]

God, the maker, from the death of sin, raises us to a new life in Christ towards the cosmos for a new life and relationship. Christ gives us nourishment, keeping us from falling and setting us in the presence of God's glory through the process of creation. Holy Spirit, the power of our life, gives us the resilience to build communities and relationships of love.

May the blessing of God, the Parent, the Son, and the Holy Spirit be among us and remain with us always, towards being a community of resilience and resistance for Justice, Peace and Integrity, now and forever. **Amen.**

---

[1] *By Chrisida Anandan*

14

Symbolic Act:
Call to Do Justice and Build Peace[1]

(As the music is played, five volunteers representing the five elements, water, sky, fire, air and earth, shall come forward and invite the congregation to partner with the elements in realising their dreams. All five volunteers shall carry an item related to the element they represent.)

Water: I the water have a dream.

A dream to flow to the deserts,

The deserts created by selfishness and exploitation.

I hear the cries of thirst, the thirst to live; the unquenchable thirst for life.

Will my dream come true?

Sky: Listen to my dream, the dream of the sky.

I dream a day will come; a day to say 'I do not

---

have horizons.'
When all that I see from here pains me.
I pray that they shall have feathers to fly beyond
the horizons to which they limit themselves to.
Will my dream come true?

Fire: I am the fire, and I too have a dream…
A dream to warm the cold minds.
Cold because, they are dead, dead to the realities
of life.
I feel the need to warm, to warm such minds
so that life sustains.
Will my dream come true?

Air: I am the air, and I too have a dream.
A dream that others will dream of me.
A dream that will never pollute me.
Because, only then I can dream to sustain their
dreams.
Will my dream come true?

Earth: I the earth also have a dream.
A dream to hold all that breathe and do not
breathe.
When my children fight for peace and space, I
cry,
Look for space not upon me, but among and
within you and then, only then can I hold You
together.
Will my dream come true?

People: **We have a dream.**
Life where justice and peace would triumph

Where the wolf shall live with the lamb
When leopards shall lie down with the kids
Where the cow and the bear shall graze
Where justice shall flow down like rivers
Where righteousness like an ever-flowing stream.

Together: This is a dream to Life. This is a dream to "Shalom"

Will our dream come true? Yes. Our dream will come true.

15

Symbolic Act: I the Lord Your God[1]
God's Lament and Our Response

I, the Lord your God, see segregated and divided communities that hurt each other and build high walls instead of reaching out with kindness and love. I see hatred and hostility in the name of religion, violence in the name of caste and gender. I see my people crying out. I feel their pain. Whom shall I send, and who will go for us?

Here I am Lord, is it I Lord?
I have heard You calling in the night
I will go, Lord, If You lead me
I will hold Your people in my heart.

I, the Lord your God, see terror threats and wars, innocent people dying as victims of brutal terrorist attacks. Many are wounded in these acts of inhuman violence: children, young and old. I'm tired of the unwillingness to see this as an urgent issue. I'm tired of those in power who work to prevent any real change. I'm tired of those who say that gun violence can't be

---

[1] *From the Church of South India Synod Session 2020 Liturgy*

reduced. I am also angry at the seeming powerlessness of our community to prevent this. I'm outraged at the selfish financial interests who block change. I see my people crying out. I feel their pain. Whom shall I send, and who will go for us?
Here I am Lord, is it I Lord?

I, the Lord your God, see the pain and suffering of children, especially those who are physically, mentally, emotionally and intellectually challenged. Women are being abused and raped, the elderly being discarded and excluded, youth going astray and are indulging in habits that harm themselves. I am also angry at the seeming powerlessness of our community to prevent this. I see my people crying out. I feel their pain. Whom shall I send, and who will go for us?
Here I am Lord, is it I Lord?

I, the Lord your God, see the pain and suffering of the refugee and migrant communities. People displaced due to war and calamities, the widening gap between the rich and the poor, the haves and the have-nots, as well as human pain and misery; I am also angry at the seeming powerlessness of our community to prevent this. I see my people crying out. I feel their pain. Whom shall I send, and who will go for us?
Here I am Lord, is it I Lord?

I, the Lord your God, see the pain and suffering of creation. I see destruction and exploitation of the earth's natural resources, and the extinction of plants and animals, endangered by human greed and your ignorance of my sacramental presence in nature; I am also angry at the seeming powerlessness of our community to prevent this. I see my people crying out. I feel their pain.

Whom shall I send, and who will go for us?

Here I am Lord, is it I Lord?

I, the Lord your God, see the Church not concerned about world peace but instead engrossed with the wealth and glamour of the Church. Not worried about justice but instead encrypted with issues of doctrinal differences and faith traditions, not concerned about establishing peace and reconciliation but instead enshrined with hegemonic structures and practices. I see my people crying out. I feel their pain. Whom shall I send, and who will go for us?

Here I am Lord, is it I Lord?

Act of Commitment

God's love through the cross calls us to a life of kenosis. It reminds us that in self-emptying ourselves, we find meaning to the fullness of life promised by Christ. So let us hold the clay jars with stains on it in our hands and empty the water in it by pouring it in the cup of our neighbour until the end of the row.

The stained clay pots symbolise our state of sinfulness and the water in it signifies God's outpouring love. As we pour water into our neighbour's pot, we are reminded about the self-emptying love of Christ on the cross; we cannot hold back or contain this love which ought to be shared with others. Amen

(As the music is played the stewards will draw water from the clay urn kept beside the cross at the altar and bring it to the congregation. The person who receives the water at the end of the row is requested to pour the water on the plant kept beside, and the congregation is requested to engage in this act prayerfully.)

———————

HYMNS

1

Arise, Arise Immanuels[1]

The annuals of this world of ours
Are filled with bitter memory
Of wars and batters raging on
The shouts and cry of humankind,

Chorus   Arise, Arise, Immanuels
                Be channels of God's peace on earth

The death knells of creation ring
O mortals, hear her groaning
Life in its fullness seeking
Called as Immanuels to this end.   **Chorus**

---

[1] *Text by Allan Samuel Palanna, set to the tune of "O Come, O Come, Emmanuel," Translator: J. M. Neale*
Tune: Veni Emmanuel (Chant)

We hear, O Lord, your voice of hope
Proclaiming justice, peace on earth
Called to be partners of your reign
Immanuels in the midst of death.   **Chorus**

———————————

2

Rejoice in Thanksgiving[1]

Rejoice in thanksgiving, give praises to our God
For all God's done and going to do in and through us
Lift up your heart, lift up your voice
Rejoice again let's all give thanks

Jesus the Lord is near to all who call His name
For in our low estate through Him we all have hope
Lift up your heart, lift up your voice
Rejoice again let's all give praise

Now as we worship God, in spirit and in truth
Let's all believe that we are called to bring a change
Lift up your heart, lift up your voice
Rejoice again let's all rejoice

---

[1] *Text by Yajenlemla Chang, set to the tune of "Rejoice the Lord is King,"
text by Charles Wesley and music by John Darwall*

3

Mary Did You Know?[1]

Mary did you know
What your world would say
If you say "Yes" to your God?
Mary did you know
What they'll make of you
If you hold on to God's word?
Did you know you'll be scorned and mocked for offerin' up
your womb?
And yet you walked that road of pain, doubt and fear

Through me will come a man
Who will bring to all
Peace, goodwill and justice
He will shame the proud
Proclaim liberty, breaking chains made by men

---

[1] *Text by Arvind Theodore, set to the of "Mary Did You Know?," text by Mark Lowry and music by Buddy Greene (Arrangement: Pentatonix)*

Did you know that I made this choice so change could be at hand?
And here's my song to sing now
A song of praise to God

O can you hear my song?
My soul will sing, My spirit rejoices
In God who is my saviour
He lifts the lowly, He fills the hungry
He shall do great things

We are called to be mothers of God
For God's in need of being born
We are called to be mothers of God
To witness a new heav'n and earth
Would we do, do what Mary did with courage, hope, and faith?
Let Christ the Son of God be born in our lives today

———————————

4

Once in Royal Indian Cities[1]

Once in Royal Indian Cities
Women had a lowly state
Where a woman taught her baby
To respect and honour all
Mother had great dreams and hopes
For Nirbhaya her little child

Men came down and crushed all her dreams
Who were like a father figure
And their gaze was a terror
And their hand was a razor
With their powerful mighty body
Raped the little child, Asifa/Priyanka

[1] *Text by Moses Shanthi Kumar Bollam John, set to the tune of "Once in Royal David's City," text by Cecil Frances Alexander and music by Henry John Gauntlett.*

And our eyes have seen the body,
Torched and body burnt alive
For that child so dear and gentle
Is no longer on the earth
But her blood is crying on
Crying out for social justice.

———————————

5

God Sent Her Call,
to be Her Witnesses

God sent Her Call, to be Her witnesses
She calls to love, live and follow
Our Easter faith She bids to live out
An empty tomb, a sign of hope, my Saviour lives.

Chorus Because he rose, we will be God's witness
Because he rose, our hope is on.
Because he rose, yes He rose
He's not entombed God,
Nor is he enthroned in heaven, but lives in us.

How can tomb hold, a new born Jesus
Who gives new hope and life to all

---

[1] *Text by Moses Shanthi Kumar Bollam John, set to the tune of "Because He lives," text and music by Gloria Gaither and Bill Gaither.*

But greater still the calm assurance
That death can't say, the final word, because he lives   **Chorus**
And now with faith, we'll move the mountains
We'll roll the stones away with faith
And then as Christ gives hope in despair
We're called to live our Easter Faith, because he lives. **Chorus**

———————————

6

God Whose Image[1]

O God, whose image with which we all experiment,
Ascribing notions that are in nature, dominant;
We miss the mark of seeing you as vulnerable,
a God who partakes in the brokenness of us all.

Burnt offerings, or calves, or even a thousand rams,
Will not for surely please God, whose image we've tainted;
Forgive us as we dictate terms for you to be revealed,
According to our comforts and structures we have built.

Reveal yourself O God in the midst of the unknown,
The strange, and bizarre spaces where we seek you no more;
Open our eyes to discern your all enabling presence,
In all of your creation forever, ever more.

---

[1] *Text by Wesley P. Kuruvilla, set to the tune of the hymn "Stand up, Stand up for Jesus," text by George Duffield and music by George J. Webb.*

7

God, We Come to Your Presence[1]

God, we come to Your presence seeking,
Gift of conscience and understanding,
That the Church be not pompous and haughty,
Where it keeps fences, firm, fixed and faulty;
Abode for all, can the Church be?

Chorus   God, may we seek courage to step up for those
in need,
Garlanding lives with love, justice, peace;
God, may we have open doors for our Churches
so to
Favour those plunged in the floods of the times.

God we desire that Church be Christ-like,
Healing, journ'ying with people in need;

---

[1] *Text by Wesley P. Kuruvilla, set to the tune of "Shine Jesus Shine," composed by Graham Kendrick.*

Not as houses of power and glory,
Nor as seats of wealth and authority;
Abode for all, may the Church be.   **Chorus**

———————————

8

When We Hear the Cry for Peace[1]

When we hear the cry for peace
Do not haste but do justice
Call is not to compromise
With the powers that demonise
Bear the cross of Lord Jesus
Break the world of injustice.

As the woman; broke the law
Swam across the status' flow
Flouting rules and passing all
Waiting not to hear a call
Dared to touch the Jewish stole
What a move to reach the "Whole"!

---

[1] *Text by Viji Varghese Eapen, set to the tune of "Rock of Ages," composed by Augustus Toplady.*

Look to Jesus, Lord who healed
One who hear His people's plead
Fighting-cries, we need to heed
"Bridging gaps" let be our creed
"Crossing bridges" let us breed
No more laws let kill this seed.

———————————

9

This Day, to You,
We Come, O Lord[1]

This day, to You, we come, O Lord
Pilgrims, to praise and preach Your Word
Gladly we come to Your presence
May You fill us with holiness.
Master, cleanse us by Your dear hand,
It's for Your service that we stand.
To You we owe, for what we are
To You we come, for what to be.

This day, to You, we come, O Lord
Pilgrims, to hear and share Your Word
Humbly we come as earthen pots,
May You fill us with Your purpose.
Renew Your spirit within us.

---

[1] *Text by Viji Varghese Eapen, set to the tune of "Sweet Hour of Prayer," text by W. W. Walford and music by William B. Bradbury.*

Hold us and mould us with kindness.
To You we owe, for what we are
To You we come, for what to be.

This day, to You, we come, O Lord
Pilgrims to claim, proclaim Your Word
Firmly we come, to seek Your face
May You fill us with all Your grace.
This Church to which we all belong
May all the days be Yours, we long.
To You we owe, for what we are
To You we come, for what to be.

———————————

10

No More We Live in World of Peace[1]

No more we live in world of peace,
No more we have a breathing space.
Valley of bones we see around,
Craving to live and move around.

Chorus   Our hope is built on Christ, the Peace
All other ground is sinking sand;
All other ground is sinking sand.

Our people long for days of peace
Our people cry for Your justice
Speak to us, God, now speak to us
Speak through us, God, now speak through us.   **Chorus**

---

[1] *Text by Viji Varghese Eapen, set to the tune of "My Hope is Built on Nothing Less," text by Edward Mote and music by William B. Bradbury.*

Come let us beat our swords to ploughs
And beat our spears to pruning hooks
To lift the world from groaning days,
To wipe the tears from mourning face.   **Chorus**

11

O Come, All Ye Peaceful[1]

O come, all ye, peaceful,
Powerful and insurgent!
O come ye, O come ye to end fascism.
Come and catch hold them—
Born to hate and fragment.
O come, let us resist them (3)
Lest, we be lost.

Blood of blood,
Breath of breath,
Lo! We belong to the Indian womb.
No more the fascists—
Forces that divide us.
O come, let us resist them (3)
Lest, we be lost.

---

[1] *Text by Viji Varghese Eapen, set to the tune of "O Come, All Ye Faithful," text by (attributed to) John Francis, translated by Frederick Oakeley, and tune Adeste Fideles.*

Shout, raise your voices,
Protect constitution,
Shout all ye citizens to save our nation.
Glory of India
Dies at hands of fascists.
O come, let us resist them (3)
Lest, we be lost.

Yea, all we greet you,
Salam! Santhi! Shalom!
Peace, love and harmony, justice for all.
Weird and the absurd,
Those who spew all hatred.
O come, let us resist them (3)
Lest, we be lost.

———————————

12

Were You There When They Found it Hard to Breathe?[1]

Were You there when they found it hard to breathe?
Were You there when they found it hard to breathe?
Oh, sometimes it causes me to tremble, tremble, tremble.
Were You there when they found it hard to breathe?

Were You there when we knelt and prayed for them?
Were You there when we knelt and prayed for them?
Oh, sometimes it causes me to tremble, tremble, tremble.
Were You there when we knelt and prayed for them?

Were You there when our faith nor work saved them?
Were You there when our faith nor work saved them?
Oh, sometimes it causes me to tremble, tremble, tremble.
Were You there when our faith nor work saved them?

---

[1] *Text by Viji Varghese Eapen, set to the tune of "Were You There When They Crucified My Lord?," source: African-American Spiritual*

Were You there when they left this world alone?
Were You there when they left this world alone?
Oh, sometimes it causes me to tremble, tremble, tremble.
Were You there when they left this world alone?

Were You there when they're thrown to fire and grave?
Were You there when they're thrown to fire and grave?
Oh, sometimes it causes me to tremble, tremble, tremble.
Were You there when they're thrown to fire and grave?

Were You there when their loved ones grieved and wept?
Were You there when their loved ones grieved and wept?
Oh, sometimes it causes me to tremble, tremble, tremble.
Were You there when their loved ones grieved and wept?

———————————

13

Broken, Shattered, Left Ov'rpowered[1]

Broken, shattered, left ov'rpowered
Seeing humanity decline
Pain and grief were thrust upon us
Joy vanished to be no more
Death gave life to fear, anxiety
Wondered if our time had come
Clung to hope like child grasps mother
While each day we drudged along.

Sick, poor, migrants, aged, and homeless
Faced the brunt of brutal loss
Did God cause it? Can God stop it?
Our minds probed with fleeting doubt
Where was God in all this suffering?

---

[1] *Text by Arvind Theodore, set to the tune of "Love Divine, All Loves Excelling," text by Charles Wesley, and Tune: Beecher (8.7.8.7 D), composed by John Zundel.*

Had God's mighty right hand failed?
Through each passing love persisted
Life survived against all odds

Streets abandoned; doors not opened
Hearts were parched as gatherings ceased
Faith being tested turned to action
Care, compassion knew no bounds
Church no longer was confined by
Boundaries, altars, and priesthood
Church as event sprung all over
Paving way for love to live

14

The Church as Event
is a Living Church of God[1]

The Church as Event is a living Church of God
The Church is where we gather to worship God of love
The Son has sacrificed life and offered life for all
The Spirit leads and heals us, from death, disease and death

The Church will manifest the full glory of our God
In bodies of all people, with hearts and minds in love
The Church will direct us to new life and life to all
Renewing every mind, and sustaining every breath.

Though we are broken-hearted, children of our God
Protect, respect and honour the life we share in love.
We come around the table with gifts, songs, prayers for all
We come to mend the broken, choosing life over death.

---

[1] *Concept: Cláudio Carvalhaes, Text by Moses Shanthi Kumar Bollam John, set to the tune of "The Church's One Foundation," text by S. J. Stone, and tune Aurelia (7.6.7.6.D) composed by Samuel S. Wesley.*

The calling is to be oriented by our God
Our streets are full of life and protesting out of love
The Church should care for all earth and none is spared at all
Let's strive for justice, freedom, equality and health.

15

Give Us Today Our Daily Bread[1]

Give us today our daily bread,
Teach us today to thank on what we're fed,
Help us today, realise many go to bed,
Without a meal and are nearly dead.

Chorus   Food for thought, food for life and food for all,
Good for thought, good for life and good for all,
Said our thought, said for life and said for all,
Live our thought, live for life and live for all.

Forgive us O God for we eat in greed,
For selfishness is what we breed,
Forgetting that sharing should be our creed,
Forever we are insensitive to those in need.   **Chorus**

---

[1] *Text and music by Raj Bharat Patta*

O God, the maker & the giver of life,
You have sent your son as bread of life,
Broken for us to save from death & strife,
Promising those that taste you, eternal life.   **Chorus**

Is starvation swallowed up in victory of sharing?
Its sting, accumulation broken by caring,
Root of greed is uprooted in that sharing,
Food for all and life for all will be its bearing.   **Chorus**

16

Thy Kingdom Come[1]

When the world's torn apart
Thy Kingdom come
When peace has lost its heart
Thy Kingdom come
When nations rise against a nation
Thy Kingdom come
When humans destroy God's creation
Thy Kingdom come

When North-South Koreas mend
Thy Kingdom come
When bombs on Syria end
Thy Kingdom come
When Windrush people's justice granted
Thy Kingdom come

---

[1] *Text and music by Raj Bharat Patta*

When Israel-Palestine are free
Thy Kingdom come

When excluded are included
Thy Kingdom come
When discrimination's uprooted
Thy Kingdom come
When oppressed are liberated
Thy Kingdom come
When unloved are forever embraced
Thy Kingdom come

Thy Kingdom will come
When we mend our broken world
Thy Kingdom will come
When we let go selfish world
Thy Kingdom will come
When we are just and be bold
Thy Kingdom will come
When our lives in Christ unfold

17

Who Knows the Pains of Deep Blue Waters

Who knows the pains of deep blue waters,
For her tears wept and kept within
What's for a man but domination that matters
For his power swept and crept herein

When she tries to quench the thirst of the poor,
He grabs it from their mouths for sure
For he dictates that water is for money and not for any
And pours her in the rich houses for waste

Arise O waters, Arise O people,
Water for life and water for all
Injustice to water and injustice to people
Speak out and speak aloud

---

[1] *Text and music by Raj Bharat Patta*

For man's injustice to be watered away
And justice to be for waters again
Let waters roll down in justice and
And let the streams be ever flowing to all in righteousness.

————————————

18

We are the Church[1]

We are the Church, You are the One we search
We 're on the march, for you are our life's approach
We bear the Cross and overcome our sins reproach
We 're in your reign living the values in perch

Chorus   Caste or Christ, make a choice now
One gives death and other lets live
To cast out caste, come let us vow
The spirit of our calling lets re-live

Divisions, discriminations and oppressions
Dominations, admonitions and suppressions
O caste, how cruel are your descriptions
Found within and around our inscriptions   **Chorus**

---

[1] *Text and music by Raj Bharat Patta*

Let justice roll down like a river
Cleansing away injustices forever
Let righteousness flow down to revere
Cleaving up the divisions sever   **Chorus**

Come out to celebrate inclusivity
Come back to life burying exclusivity
Call out to fight darkness in all sincerity
Call out a fast for it's a gain to liberty   **Chorus**

————————————

Afterword

*Ferdinand Anno**

The liturgical resources in this collection echo so much of the pathos, hopes, struggles and faith of those who are often concealed, if not made invisible, in the texts and rubrics of our liturgical establishments. This is true of Christianity in general. The history of Christianity as Christendom is a history of centralisation, and consequentially of marginalisation and exclusion. This history was one hegemonic process of empire-building aimed at maintaining the centre's control over the marginal subaltern majority. In this process of hegemonisation and homogenisation where societies' "discourses of consent" are controlled and regulated by the dominant discourse, the ruling powers also consolidate themselves in positions of authority and power.

The consolidation of the centre through the silencing of dissenting theological and liturgical voices effectively established orthodox Christianity and laid down the institutional base of what would be the cultural, spiritual and political colonisation of many societies from centuries of Roman imperial rule to the most recent waves of missionary conquests. In this process of hegemonisation, the liturgy plays an ideological role. In all its static and dynamic objectivations, the liturgy became an important instrument in the institutionalisation and sacralisation of the centre. Public worship and popular devotion being the primary formators of Christian culture, spirituality and religious discourse, the control of the liturgy thus was crucial to the powers that be. Through the liturgical rite, the empire found its most potent means of self-communication and self-rationalisation. In and through the liturgies consenting to and helping build hegemonic discourse, Christendom re-formed Christianity to provide the empire with its most dependable and sustainable lasting religio-cultural and cultic base.

In our contemporary world, Christendom has taken a new form in the alliance of Church interests with contemporary empire-building. In this neo-Christendom Church, the liturgy maintains an ambiguous yet ultimately consenting, collaborative and ideological stance vis-à-vis the establishment. As in Christendom, the rites of contemporary establishment Christianity serve as a continuing religious rationalisation and sacralisation of the imperial structures of Church and society. It is in this context that this collection is resistance. It is in this context that the liturgical pieces are a transgression of an inherited tradition that has put more emphasis on tradition rather than traditioning—where the holy resides not in liturgical orthopraxy but in the celebration of an ongoing salvific event among those who need God the most.

The pieces in this collection reflect and echo what the editor words as "manyness" and "marginality" specifically in the South Asian context. No longer is worship among the subaltern majority a simple representation of imperial images and designs. Post-Christendom subaltern worship has deconstructed liturgical establishments or the liturgical re-presentations of imperial symbolic representations. Further, challenging our complacencies regarding our projects in decolonialisation, liturgical establishments in this volume are described by the editor as spanning a wide spectrum from colonial worship to mainstream ecumenical liturgies, extending even to those that are now touted in many circles as success stories in the nationalisation and indigenisation of worship. This is nowhere truer than in the South Asian context where elitist nationalist theologies and Christian praxis have been for a long period mainstreamed and looked up to as the Asian alternative.

The intent is, however clear, the critique offered in these liturgies allows for a more profound encounter and engagement with divinity in the margins of contemporary empire-building. We can see this volume as a correspondent with developments in Christian arts in the Asian scene, particularly in the sphere of Christological re-imagination and deconstruction. Like their counterparts in the visual arts, these liturgies of resistance exhibit multiple expressions of the celebration of the gospel; and that this gospel is being constructed from different experiences of marginality involving caste, class, gender, ethnicity, the physically challenged, among others.

The ritualed externalisation of this encounter with manyness and marginality can, potentially, provide a spiritual centre for mass dissent where the masses and the marginalised are enabled to construct and evolve a new mythography for their emancipation. Like in contemporary Asian Christian arts that owe their power and efficacy to their capacity to visually mediate and communicate divine presence and messages that speak prophetically in our time, these liturgies of resistance serve as the theo-graphical and theological impetus for mass emancipatory politics. Resistance liturgies' imagination of the dissident God-in-Christ in particular sets in motion dissident energies to subvert and transgress the social, economic, cultural and religious structures that maintain today's empire.

If the liturgies and icons of colonial Christianity were able to nourish a spirituality of reaction, then a parallel role for the liturgies of resistance such as these in the collection can, in as powerful ways, serve as the lifeblood of revolution towards social reversal. The cult and arts of Christendom had, for a long time, effectively kept powerful in their places and the poor, the othered, and marginalised in their wretchedness. Through the same medium can the social cancer of homogenisation and marginalisation be corrected: from the re-Christianisation of the public imagination in the tradition of the dissident Christ to mass upheavals. Here, the popular cult and Christology of colonial subjects come to mind when, in several national histories, they effectively nourished the revolutionary spirituality of the inarticulate mass to launch social upheavals that inaugurated anti-colonial struggles all over the colonised world.

Viji Varghese Eapen has correctly placed the liturgical pieces in the *limen* betwixt home, i.e. "manyness" and "marginality," and the vestiges of colonial Christianity and its representations. This is where this volume locates itself, at the *limen* between the old and the new where liturgical imagination does the difficult process of navigating through the Scylla and Charybdis of liturgical deconstruction.

The pieces reflect this location. They are "homework" in progress and are texts and rubrics in search of a more dynamic kind of ritual home that is indigenous to their laments, hopes and resolve to liturgically create that new and just world. These dissident liturgies even in their liminal location all lead to the ritualisation of peoples' theologies of resistance. They witness to the continuing relevance of the liturgy in the reordering of the cosmos, in the construction of a new world, and the birthing of new life.

* **Dr Ferdinand Anno** serves as Professor of Theology, Liturgy, and the Arts at the Union Theological Seminary, Philippines.